CONTENTS

BREAKFAST **8**

    1. Basil Tomato Frittata 8

    2. Italian Breakfast Frittata 8

    3. Healthy Baked Omelette 8

    4. Easy Egg Casserole 9

    5. Flavor Packed Breakfast Casserole 10

    6. Vegetable Sausage Egg Bake 10

    7. Cheese Broccoli Bake 11

    8. Cheese Ham Omelette 11

    9. Eggs in Avocado Cups 11

    10. Cinnamon French Toasts 12

    11. Sweet Spiced Toasts 12

    12. Savory French Toast 13

    13. Cheddar Mustard Toasts 14

    14. Pickled Toasts 14

    15. Ricotta Toasts with Salmon 14

    16. Pumpkin Pancakes 15

    17. Quick Cheese Omelet 15

    18. Tomato Spinach Frittata 16

    19. Ham Egg Brunch Bake 16

    20. Roasted Brussels Sprouts & Sweet Potatoes 17

    21. Roasted Potato Wedges 17

    22. Breakfast Egg Bites 17

    23. Mushroom & Pepperoncini Omelet 18

    24. Chicken Omelet 18

    25. Chicken & Zucchini Omelet 19

    26. Pepperoni Omelet 19

    27. Sausage Omelet 20

    28. Pancetta & Hot Dogs Omelet 20

    29. Egg & Tofu Omelet 21

    30. Eggs, Tofu & Mushroom Omelet 21

    31. Eggs in Bread & Bacon Cups 22

    32. Spinach & Mozzarella Muffins 22

    33. Bacon & Spinach Muffins 23

    34. Ham Muffins 23

    35. Savory Carrot Muffins 24

Beef, Lamb & Pork Recipes **26**

    36. Saucy beef bake 26

    37. Parmesan meatballs 26

    38. Tricolor beef skewers 27

    39. Yogurt beef kebabs 27

    40. Agave beef kebabs 28

    41. Beef skewers with potato salad 28

    42. Classic souvlaki kebobs 29

    43. Harissa dipped beef skewers 29

    44. Onion pepper beef kebobs 30

    45. Mayo spiced kebobs 30

46. Beef with orzo salad 31
47. Beef zucchini shashliks 32
48. Spiced beef skewers 32
49. Cheeseburger Egg Rolls 33
50. Air Fried Grilled Steak 33
51. Juicy Cheeseburgers 33
52. Spicy Thai Beef Stir-Fry 34
53. Beef Brisket Recipe from Texas 35
54. Copycat Taco Bell Crunch Wraps 35
55. Steak and Mushroom Gravy 35
56. Air Fryer Beef Casserole 36
57. Asian Inspired Sichuan Lamb 37
58. Garlic and Rosemary Lamb Cutlets 37
59. Garlic Sauced Lamb Chops 38
60. Herb Encrusted Lamb Chops 38
61. Herbed Rack of Lamb 39
62. Lamb Roast with Root Vegetables 39
63. Lemon and Cumin Coated Rack of Lamb 40
64. Macadamia Rack of Lamb 41
65. Bacon-Wrapped Pork Tenderloin 41
66. Dijon Garlic Pork Tenderloin 42
67. Pork Neck with Salad 42
68. Chinese Braised Pork Belly 43
69. Air Fryer Sweet and Sour Pork 44
70. Juicy Pork Ribs Ole 44
71. Teriyaki Pork Rolls 45
72. Barbecue Flavored Pork Ribs 45
73. Rustic Pork Ribs 46
74. Italian Parmesan Breaded Pork Chops 46
75. Crispy Breaded Pork Chops 46
76. Caramelized Pork Shoulder 47
77. Roasted Pork Tenderloin 47
78. Bacon Wrapped Pork Tenderloin 48
79. Dijon Garlic Pork Tenderloin 48
80. Pork Neck with Salad 49
81. Chinese Braised Pork Belly 50
82. Air Fryer Sweet and Sour Pork 50
83. Juicy Pork Ribs Ole 51
POULTRY RECIPES **52**
84. Deviled chicken 52
85. Marinated chicken parmesan 52
86. Rosemary lemon chicken 53
87. Garlic chicken potatoes 53
88. Chicken potato bake 54
89. Spanish chicken bake 54
90. Chicken pasta bake 55
91. Creamy chicken casserole 56
92. Italian chicken bake 56
93. Pesto chicken bake 57

94. Baked duck..57
95. Roasted goose 58
96. Christmas roast goose 58
97. Honey and Wine Chicken Breasts 59
98. Crispy Honey Garlic Chicken Wings 59
99. Lemon-Pepper Chicken Wings..59
100. Cheesy Chicken in Leek-Tomato Sauce 60
101. Mexican Chicken Burgers 61
102. Fried Chicken Livers 61
103. Minty Chicken-Fried Pork Chops 61
104. Crispy Southern Fried Chicken 62
105. Tex-Mex Turkey Burgers 63
106. Air Fryer Turkey Breast 63
107. Mustard Chicken Tenders 63
108. Chicken Nuggets 64
109. Cheesy Chicken Fritters 64
110. Air Fryer Chicken Parmesan 65
111. Pretzel Crusted Chicken With Spicy Mustard Sauce 65
112. Chinese-Style Sticky Turkey Thighs..66
113. Easy Hot Chicken Drumsticks 67
114. Crunchy Munchy Chicken Tenders With Peanuts........................67

FISH AND SEAFOOD RECIPES 68
115. Prawn Momo's Recipe 68
116. Fish club Classic Sandwich..68
117. Prawn Fried Baked Pastry 69
118. Fish Spicy Lemon Kebab 69
119. Fish Oregano Fingers 70
120. Prawn Grandma's Easy to Cook Wontons 71
121. Tuna Sandwich...71
122. Salmon Tandoor 72
123. Carp Best Homemade Croquette 72
124. Shrimp Momo's Recipe 73
125. Salmon fries...74
126. Oyster Club Sandwich 74
127. Cheese Carp Fries..75
128. Seafood Pizza 75
129. Prawn Momo's Recipe 76
130. Fish Club Classic Sandwich 76
131. Prawn Fried Baked Pastry 77
132. Fish Spicy Lemon Kebab 78
133. Fish Oregano Fingers 78
134. Prawn Grandma's Easy to Cook Wontons 79
135. Tuna Sandwich...79
136. Scallops And Spring Veggies 80
137. Air Fryer Salmon Patties 81
138. Salmon Noodles 81
139. Beer-battered fish and chips..81
140. Tuna Stuffed Potatoes 82
141. Fried Calamari 83

142. Soy And Ginger Shrimp 83
143. Crispy Cheesy Fish Fingers 83

VEGETABLES RECIPES **85**

144. Crispy Brussels Sprouts 85
145. Flatbread 85
146. Creamy Cabbage 85
147. Creamy Potatoes 86
148. Green Beans And Cherry Tomatoes 86
149. Crispy Brussels Sprouts And Potatoes 86
150. Herbed Tomatoes 87
151. Air Fried Leeks 87
152. Crispy Broccoli 87
153. Garlic-Roasted Bell Peppers 88
154. Asparagus With Garlic 88
155. Cheesy Roasted Sweet Potatoes 88
156. Mushroom and Feta Frittata 89
157. Cauliflower pizza crust 89
158. Olives and artichokes 89
159. Lemon asparagus 90
160. Savory cabbage and tomatoes 90
161. Pecan brownies 90
162. Cheesy endives 91
163. Cauliflower steak 91
164. Parmesan Broccoli and Asparagus 92
165. Air Fryer Crunchy Cauliflower 92
166. Air Fryer Veg Buffalo Cauliflower 92
167. Air Fryer Asparagus 93
168. Almond Flour Battered and Crisped Onion Rings 93
169. Air Fryer Buffalo Cauliflower 93
170. Air Fryer Kale Chips 94
171. Air Fried Mozzarella Stalks 94
172. Air Fryer Vegan Fried Ravioli 95
173. Air Fryer Veg Pizza 96
174. Air Fryer Buffalo Cauliflower – Onion Dip 96

APPETIZERS RECIPES **98**

175. Steamed Pot Stickers 98
176. Beef and Mango Skewers 98
177. Curried Sweet Potato Fries 99
178. Spicy Kale Chips with Yogurt Sauce 99
179. Phyllo Artichoke Triangles 100
180. Arancini 100
181. Steamed Pot Stickers 101
182. Beef and Mango Skewers 101
183. Curried Sweet Potato Fries 102
184. Spicy Kale Chips with Yogurt Sauce 102
185. Phyllo Artichoke Triangles 103
186. Arancini 103
187. Pesto Bruschetta 104
188. Fried Tortellini with Spicy Dipping Sauce 104

189. Peanut Butter Banana Bread...105
190. Chocolate Banana Bread..105
191. Allspice Chicken Wings..106
192. Friday Night Pineapple Sticky Ribs...107
193. Egg Roll Wrapped With Cabbage And Prawns...107
194. Sesame Garlic Chicken Wings..108
195. Savory Chicken Nuggets With Parmesan Cheese...108
196. Butternut Squash With Thyme...109
197. Chicken Breasts In Golden Crumb...109
198. Yogurt Chicken Tacos..109
199. Flawless Kale Chips...110
200. Cheese Fish Balls..110

DESSERT RECIPES **111**
201. Angel Food Cake...111
202. Apple Pie in Air Fryer...111
203. Apple-Toffee Upside-Down Cake..112
204. Banana-Choco Brownies...112
205. Blueberry & Lemon Cake...113
206. Bread Pudding with Cranberry..113
207. Cherries 'n Almond Flour Bars..114
208. Cherry-Choco Bars..114
209. Chocolate Chip in a Mug..115
210. Choco-Peanut Mug Cake..115
211. Coco-Lime Bars...115
212. Coconut 'n Almond Fat Bombs..116
213. Coconutty Lemon Bars..116
214. Coffee 'n Blueberry Cake..117
215. Date & Walnut Bread...117
216. Brown Sugar Banana Bread..118
217. Cinnamon Banana Bread...119
218. Banana & Walnut Bread...119
219. Banana & Raisin Bread..120
220. 3-Ingredients Banana Bread...121
221. Yogurt Banana Bread...121
222. Sour Cream Banana Bread..122
223. Peanut Butter Banana Bread...122
224. Cinnamon & Honey Apples With Hazelnuts...123
225. Pan-Fried Bananas...123
226. Delicious Banana Pastry With Berries...124
227. Easy Mocha Cake...124
228. Choco Lava Cakes..124
229. Mouthwatering Chocolate Soufflé...125
230. Maple Pecan Pie..125
231. Tangerine Cake..126
232. Blueberry Pudding...126
233. Cocoa And Almond Bars...126
234. Chocolate And Pomegranate Bars...127
235. Tomato Cake..127
236. Berries Mix...128

237. Passion Fruit Pudding...128
238. Air Fried Apples..128
239. Pumpkin Cookies 129
240. Figs And Coconut Butter Mix 129
241. Lemon Bars..130
242. Orange Sponge Cake 130
243. Cashew Bars...130
244. Fried Cream..131
245. Apple, cream, and hazelnut crumble 131
246. Fregolotta with hazelnuts 132
247. Apple Treat With Raisins...132
248. Almond Cookies With Dark Chocolate..132
249. Air Fried Banana With Sesame Seeds 133
250. Vanilla Brownies With Chocolate Chips..133

BREAKFAST

1. Basil Tomato Frittata

P Prep Time 10 m | P Cooking Time 35 m | 6 Servings

Ingredients

- 12 eggs
- 1/2 cup cheddar cheese, grated
- 1 1/2 cups cherry tomatoes, cut in half
- 1/2 cup fresh basil, chopped
- 1 cup baby spinach, chopped
- 1/2 cup yogurt
- Pepper
- Salt

Directions

1. Spray a baking dish using cooking spray and set aside.
2. Insert wire rack in rack position 6. Select bake, set temperature 390 F, timer for 35 minutes. Press start to preheat the oven.
3. Whisk eggs and yogurt inside a large bowl.
4. Layer spinach, basil, tomatoes, and cheese in prepared baking dish. Pour egg mixture over spinach mixture. Season with pepper and salt.
5. Bake in the oven for 35 minutes.
6. Serve and enjoy.

Nutrition

Calories 188 | Fat 12.2 g | Carbohydrates 4.2 g | Sugar 3.4 g | Protein 15.2 g | Cholesterol 338 mg

2. Italian Breakfast Frittata

P Prep Time 10 m | P Cooking Time 30 m | 4 Servings

Ingredients

- 8 eggs
- 1 tbsp. fresh parsley, chopped
- 3 tbsp. parmesan cheese, grated
- 2 small zucchinis, chopped and cooked
- 1/2 cup pancetta, chopped and cooked
- Pepper
- Salt

Directions

1. Spray a baking dish using cooking spray and set aside.
2. Insert wire rack in rack position 6. Select bake, set temperature 350 F, timer for 20 minutes. Press start to preheat the oven.
3. In a mixing bowl, whisk eggs with pepper and salt. Add parsley, cheese, zucchini, and pancetta and stir well.
4. Pour egg mixture into the baking dish that was prepared.
5. Bake frittata for 20 minutes.
6. Serve and enjoy.

Nutrition

Calories 327 | Fat 23.2 g | Carbohydrates 3.5 g | Sugar 1.7 g | Protein 26 g | Cholesterol 367 mg

3. Healthy Baked Omelette

P Prep Time 10 m | P Cooking Time 45 m | 6 Servings
Ingredients
- 8 eggs
- 1 cup bell pepper, chopped
- 1/2 cup onion, chopped
- 1/2 cup cheddar cheese, shredded
- 6 oz. ham, diced and cooked
- 1 cup milk
- Pepper
- Salt

Directions
1. Spray an 8-inch baking dish using cooking spray and set aside.
2. Insert wire rack in rack position 6. Select bake, set temperature 350 F, timer for 45 minutes. Press start to preheat the oven.
3. In a large bowl, whisk milk with egg, pepper, and salt. Add remaining ingredients and stir well.
4. Pour egg mixture into the baking dish that was prepared.
5. Bake omelet for 45 minutes.
6. Slice and serve.

Nutrition
Calories 199 | Fat 12.3 g | Carbohydrates 6.1 g | Sugar 3.7 g | Protein 16.1 g | Cholesterol 248 mg

4. Easy Egg Casserole

P Prep Time 10 m | P Cooking Time 55 m | 8 Servings
Ingredients
- 8 eggs
- 1/2 tsp garlic powder
- 2 cups cheddar cheese, shredded
- 1 cup milk
- 24 oz. frozen hash browns, thawed
- 1/2 onion, diced
- 1 red pepper, diced
- 4 bacon slices, diced
- 1/2 lb. turkey breakfast sausage
- Pepper
- Salt

Directions
1. Spray a 9*13-inch baking dish using cooking spray and set aside.
2. Insert wire rack in rack position 6. Select bake, set temperature 350 F, timer for 50 minutes. Press start to preheat the oven.
3. Cook the breakfast sausage in a pan over medium heat until cooked through. Drain well and set aside.
4. Cook bacon in the same pan. Drain well and keep aside.
5. In a mixing bowl, whisk eggs with milk, garlic powder, pepper, and salt. Add 1 cup cheese, hash browns, onion, red pepper, bacon, and sausage and stir well.
6. Pour the entire egg mixture into the baking dish. Sprinkle remaining cheese on top.
7. Cover dish with foil and bake for 50 minutes. Remove foil and bake for 5 more minutes.
8. Serve and enjoy.

Nutrition
Calories 479 | Fat 29.1 g | Carbohydrates 34.1 g | Sugar 4.2 g | Protein 20.2 g | Cholesterol 207 mg

5. Flavor Packed Breakfast Casserole

P Prep Time 10 m | P Cooking Time 40 m | 8 Servings
Ingredients
- 12 eggs
- 1/2 cup cheddar cheese, shredded
- 1 tsp garlic powder
- 1 cup milk
- 1/4 cup onion, diced
- 2 bell pepper, cubed
- 4 small potatoes, cubed
- 2 cups sausage, cooked and diced
- Pepper
- Salt

Directions
1. Spray a 9*13-inch baking dish using cooking spray and keep aside.
2. Insert wire rack in rack position 6. Select bake, set temperature 350 F, timer for 40 minutes. Press start to preheat the oven.
3. In a large bowl, whisk eggs with milk, garlic powder, pepper, and salt.
4. Add sausage, bell peppers, and potatoes into the baking dish. Pour egg mixture over sausage mixture. Sprinkle with cheese and onion.
5. Bake casserole for 40 minutes.
6. Slice and serve.

Nutrition
Calories 232 | Fat 11.6 g | Carbohydrates 18.3 g | Sugar 4.6 g | Protein 14.2 g | Cholesterol 261 mg

6. Vegetable Sausage Egg Bake

P Prep Time 10 m | P Cooking Time 35 m | 4 Servings
Ingredients
- 10 eggs
- 1 cup spinach, diced
- 1 cup onion, diced
- 1 cup pepper, diced
- 1 lb. sausage, cut into 1/2-inch pieces
- 1 tsp garlic powder
- 1/2 cup almond milk
- Pepper
- Salt

Directions
1. Spray an 8*8-inch baking dish with cooking spray and set aside.
2. Insert wire rack in rack position 6. Select bake, set temperature 390 F, timer for 35 minutes. Press start to preheat the oven.
3. In a bowl, whisk milk with eggs and spices. Add vegetables and sausage and stir to combine.

4. Pour the mixture of egg into the prepared baking dish. Bake for 35 minutes.
5. Slice and serve.

Nutrition

Calories 653 | Fat 50.6 g | Carbohydrates 12.6 g | Sugar 3.3 g | Protein 38.3 g | Cholesterol 504 mg

7. Cheese Broccoli Bake

P Prep Time 10 m | P Cooking Time 30 m | 12 Servings

Ingredients

- 12 eggs
- 1 1/2 cup cheddar cheese, shredded
- 2 cups broccoli florets, chopped
- 1 small onion, diced
- 1 cup milk
- Pepper
- Salt

Directions

1. Spray a 9*13-inch baking dish using cooking spray and set aside.
2. Insert wire rack in rack position 6. Select bake, set temperature 390 F, timer for 30 minutes. Press start to preheat the oven.
3. In a large bowl, whisk eggs with milk, pepper, and salt. Add cheese, broccoli, and onion and stir well.
4. Pour the mixture of eggs into the prepared baking dish and bake for 30 minutes.
5. Slice and serve.

Nutrition

Calories 138 | Fat 9.5 g | Carbohydrates 3.1 g | Sugar 1.8 g | Protein 10.2 g ||Cholesterol 180 mg

8. Cheese Ham Omelette

P Prep Time 10 m | P Cooking Time 25 m | 6 Servings

Ingredients

- 8 eggs
- 1 cup ham, chopped
- 1 cup cheddar cheese, shredded
- 1/3 cup milk
- Pepper
- Salt

Directions

1. Spray a 9*9-inch baking dish using cooking spray and set aside.
2. Insert wire rack in rack position 6. Select bake, set temperature 390 F, timer for 25 minutes. Press start to preheat the oven.
3. In a large bowl, whisk eggs with milk, pepper, and salt. Stir in ham and cheese.
4. Pour the mixture of eggs into the prepared baking dish and bake for 25 minutes.
5. Slice and serve.

Nutrition

Calories 203 | Fat 14.3 g | Carbohydrates 2.2 g | Sugar 1.2 g| Protein 16.3 g | Cholesterol 252 mg

9. Eggs in Avocado Cups

P Prep Time 10 m | P Cooking Time 10 m | 2 Servings

Ingredients:
- 1 avocado, halved and pitted
- 2 large eggs
- Salt and ground black pepper, as required
- 2 cooked bacon slices, crumbled

Directions:
1. Carefully, scoop out about 2 teaspoons of flesh from each avocado half.
2. Crack 1 egg in each avocado half and sprinkle with salt and black pepper.
3. Press "Power Button" of Air Fry Oven and turn the dial to select the "Air Roast" mode.
4. Press the Time button and again turn the dial to set the cooking time to 10 minutes.
5. Now push the Temp button and rotate the dial to set the temperature at 375 degrees F.
6. Press "Start/Pause" button to start.
7. When the unit beeps to show that it is preheated, open the lid and line the "Sheet Pan" with a lightly, grease piece of foil.
8. Arrange avocado halves into the "Sheet Pan" and insert in the oven.
9. Top each avocado half with bacon pieces and serve.

Nutrition:
Calories 300|Fat 26.6 g |Cholesterol 190 mg |Sodium 229 mg |Carbs 9 g |Fiber 6.7 g|Protein 9.7g

10. Cinnamon French Toasts

P Prep Time 10 m | P Cooking Time 5 m | 2 Servings

Ingredients:
- 2 eggs
- ¼ cup whole milk
- 3 tablespoons sugar
- 2 teaspoons olive oil
- 1/8 teaspoon vanilla extract
- 1/8 teaspoon ground cinnamon
- 4 bread slices

Directions:
1. In a large bowl, mix together all the ingredients except bread slices.
2. Coat the bread slices with egg mixture evenly.
3. Press "Power Button" of Air Fry Oven and turn the dial to select the "Air Fry" mode.
4. Press the Time button and again turn the dial to set the cooking time to 6 minutes.
5. Now push the Temp button and rotate the dial to set the temperature at 390 degrees F.
6. Press "Start/Pause" button to start.
7. When the unit beeps to show that it is preheated, open the lid and lightly, grease the sheet pan.
8. Arrange the bread slices into "Air Fry Basket" and insert in the oven.
9. Flip the bread slices once halfway through.
10. Serve warm.

Nutrition
Calories 238|Fat 10.6 g |Cholesterol 167 mg| Sodium 122 mg |Carbs 0.8 g |Fiber 0.5|Protein 7.9g

11. Sweet Spiced Toasts

P Prep Time 10 m | P Cooking Time 5 m | 3 Servings

Ingredients:
- ¼ cup sugar

- ½ teaspoon ground cinnamon
- 1/8 teaspoon ground cloves
- 1/8 teaspoon ground ginger
- ½ teaspoons vanilla extract
- ¼ cup salted butter, softened
- 6 bread slices

Directions:
1.   In a bowl, add the sugar, vanilla, cinnamon, pepper, and butter. Mix until smooth.
2.   Spread the butter mixture evenly over each bread slice.
3.   Press "Power Button" of Air Fry Oven and turn the dial to select the "Air Fry" mode.
4.   Press the Time button and again turn the dial to set the cooking time to 4 minutes.
5.   Now push the Temp button and rotate the dial to set the temperature at 400 degrees F.
6.   Press "Start/Pause" button to start.
7.   When the unit beeps to show that it is preheated, open the lid and lightly, grease the sheet pan.
8.   Arrange the bread slices into "Air Fry Basket" buttered-side up and insert in the oven.
9.   Serve warm.

Nutrition
Calories 250 | Fat 16 g| Cholesterol 41 mg |Sodium 232 mg |Carbs 26.3 g |Fiber 0.7 g| Protein 1.6 g

12. Savory French Toast

P Prep Time 10 m | P Cooking Time 5 m | 2 Servings
Ingredients:
- ¼ cup chickpea flour
- 3 tablespoons onion, finely chopped
- 2 teaspoons green chili, seeded and finely chopped
- ½ teaspoon red chili powder
- ¼ teaspoon ground turmeric
- ¼ teaspoon ground cumin
- Salt, to taste
- Water, as needed
- 4 bread slices

Directions:
1.   Add all the ingredients except bread slices in a large bowl and mix until a thick mixture form.
2.   With a spoon, spread the mixture over both sides of each bread slice.
3.   Arrange the bread slices into the lightly greased the sheet pan.
4.   Press "Power Button" of Air Fry Oven and turn the dial to select the "Air Fry" mode.
5.   Press the Time button and again turn the dial to set the cooking time to 5 minutes.
6.   Now push the Temp button and rotate the dial to set the temperature at 390 degrees F.
7.   Press "Start/Pause" button to start.
8.   When the unit beeps to show that it is preheated, open the lid and lightly, grease sheet pan.
9.   Arrange the bread slices into "Air Fry Basket" and insert in the oven.
10.   Flip the bread slices once halfway through.
11.   Serve warm.

Nutrition:

Calories 151| Fat 2.3 g |Cholesterol 0 mg |Sodium 234 mg |Carbs 26.7 g| Fiber 5.4 g|Protein 6.5g

13. Cheddar Mustard Toasts

P Prep Time 10 m | P Cooking Time 10 m | 2 Servings

Ingredients:
- 4 bread slices
- 2 tablespoons cheddar cheese, shredded
- 2 eggs, whites and yolks, separated
- 1 tablespoon mustard
- 1 tablespoon paprika

Directions:
1. In a clean glass bowl, add the egg whites in and beat until they form soft peaks.
2. In another bowl, mix together the cheese, egg yolks, mustard, and paprika.
3. Gently, fold in the egg whites.
4. Spread the mustard mixture over the toasted bread slices.
5. Press "Power Button" of Air Fry Oven and turn the dial to select the "Air Fry" mode.
6. Press the Time button and again turn the dial to set the cooking time to 10 minutes.
7. Now push the Temp button and rotate the dial to set the temperature at 355 degrees F.
8. Press "Start/Pause" button to start.
9. When the unit beeps to show that it is preheated, open the lid and lightly, grease the sheet pan.
10. Arrange the bread slices into "Air Fry Basket" and insert in the oven.
11. Serve warm.

Nutrition:
Calories 175|Fat 9.4 g|Cholesterol 171 mg|Sodium 229 mg|Carbs 13.4 g|Fiber 2.5 g|Protein10.6 g

14. Pickled Toasts

P Prep Time 10 m | P Cooking Time 5 m | 2 Servings

Ingredients:
- 4 bread slices, toasted
- 2 tablespoons unsalted butter, softened
- 2 tablespoons Branston pickle
- ¼ cup Parmesan cheese, grated

Directions:
1. Spread butter over bread slices evenly, followed by Branston pickle.
2. Top with cheese evenly.
3. Press "Power Button" of Air Fry Oven and turn the dial to select the "Air Fry" mode.
4. Press the Time button and again turn the dial to set the cooking time to 5 minutes.
5. Now push the Temp button and rotate the dial to set the temperature at 390 degrees F.
6. Press "Start/Pause" button to start.
7. When the unit beeps to show that it is preheated, open the lid and lightly, grease the sheet pan.
8. Arrange the bread slices into "Air Fry Basket" and insert in the oven.
9. Serve warm.

Nutrition:
Calories 211|Fat 14.5 g|Cholesterol 39 mg|Sodium 450 mg|Carbs 16.1 g|Fiber 0.4 g|Protein 5.5 g

15. Ricotta Toasts with Salmon

P Prep Time 10 m | P Cooking Time 4 m | 2 Servings

Ingredients:
- 4 bread slices
- 1 garlic clove, minced
- 8 oz. ricotta cheese
- 1 teaspoon lemon zest
- Freshly ground black pepper, to taste
- 4 oz. smoked salmon

Directions:
1. In a food processor, add the garlic, ricotta, lemon zest and black pepper and pulse until smooth.
2. Spread ricotta mixture over each bread slices evenly.
3. Press "Power Button" of Air Fry Oven and turn the dial to select the "Air Fry" mode.
4. Press the Time button and again turn the dial to set the cooking time to 4 minutes.
5. Now push the Temp button and rotate the dial to set the temperature at 355 degrees F.
6. Press "Start/Pause" button to start.
7. When the unit beeps to show that it is preheated, open the lid and lightly, grease the sheet pan.
8. Arrange the bread slices into "Air Fry Basket" and insert in the oven.
9. Top with salmon and serve.

Nutrition:
Calories 274|Fat 12 g|Cholesterol 48 mg|Sodium 1300 mg|Carbs 15.7 g|Fiber 0.5 g|Protein 4.8 g

16. Pumpkin Pancakes

P Prep Time 15 m | P Cooking Time 12 m | 4 Servings

Ingredients:
- 1 square puff pastry
- 3 tablespoons pumpkin filling
- 1 small egg, beaten

Directions:
1. Roll out a square of puff pastry and layer it with pumpkin pie filling, leaving about ¼-inch space around the edges.
2. Cut it up into 8 equal sized square pieces and coat the edges with beaten egg.
3. Press "Power Button" of Air Fry Oven and turn the dial to select the "Air Fry" mode.
4. Press the Time button and again turn the dial to set the cooking time to 12 minutes.
5. Now push the Temp button and rotate the dial to set the temperature at 355 degrees F.
6. Press "Start/Pause" button to start.
7. When the unit beeps to show that it is preheated, open the lid.
8. Arrange the squares into a greased "Sheet Pan" and insert in the oven.
9. Serve warm.

Nutrition:
Calories 109|Fat 6.7 g |Cholesterol 34 mg|Sodium 87 mg |Carbs 9.8 g|Fiber 0.5 g|Protein 2.4 g

17. Quick Cheese Omelet

P Prep Time 5 m | P Cooking Time 9 m | 1 Servings

Ingredients
- 2 eggs, lightly beaten
- ¼ cup cheddar cheese, shredded

- ¼ cup milk
- Pepper
- Salt

Directions
1. In a bowl, whisk milk, eggs with pepper, and salt.
2. Spray small air fryer pan with cooking spray.
3. Pour egg mixture into the prepared pan and cook at 350 F for 6 minutes.
4. Sprinkle cheese on top and cook for 3 minutes more.
5. Serve and enjoy.

Nutrition
Calories 270 | Fat 19.4 g | Carbohydrates 4.1 g | Sugar 3.6 g | Protein 20.1 g | Cholesterol 362 mg

18. Tomato Spinach Frittata

P Prep Time 10 m | P Cooking Time 7 m | 1 Servings

Ingredients
- 2 eggs, lightly beaten
- ¼ cup spinach, chopped
- ¼ cup tomatoes, chopped
- 2 tbsp. milk
- 1 tbsp. parmesan cheese, grated
- Pepper
- Salt

Directions
1. In a medium bowl, whisk eggs. Add other ingredients and mix until well combined.
2. Spray small air fryer pan with cooking spray.
3. Pour egg mixture into the prepared pan and cook at 330 F for 7 minutes.
4. Serve and enjoy.

Nutrition
Calories 189 | Fat 11.7 g | Carbohydrates 4.3 g | Sugar 3.3 g | Protein 15.7 g | Cholesterol 337 mg

19. Ham Egg Brunch Bake

P Prep Time 10 m | P Cooking Time 60 m | 6 Servings

Ingredients
- 4 eggs
- 20 oz. hash browns
- 1 onion, chopped
- 2 cups ham, chopped
- 3 cups cheddar cheese, shredded
- 1 cup sour cream
- 1 cup milk
- Pepper
- Salt

Directions
1. Spray a 9*13-inch baking dish using cooking spray and set aside.
2. Insert wire rack in rack position 6. Select bake, set temperature 375 F, timer for 35 minutes. Press start to preheat the oven.
3. In a large bowl, whisk eggs with sour cream, milk, pepper, and salt. Add 2 cups cheese and stir well.

4. Cook onion and ham in a medium pan until onion is softened.
5. Add hash brown to the pan and cook for 5 minutes.
6. Add onion ham mixture into the egg mixture and mix well.
7. Pour the mixture of eggs into the prepared baking dish. Cover dish with foil and bake for 35 minutes.
8. Remove foil and bake for 25 minutes more.
9. Slice and serve.

Nutrition

Calories 703 | Fat 46.2 g | Carbohydrates 41.2 g | Sugar 4.6 g | Protein 30.8 g | Cholesterol 214 mg

20. Roasted Brussels Sprouts & Sweet Potatoes

P Prep Time 10 m | P Cooking Time 20 m | 4 Servings

Ingredients

- 1 lb. Brussels sprouts, cut in half
- 2 sweet potatoes, wash and cut into 1-inch pieces
- 2 tbsp. olive oil
- ¼ tsp garlic powder
- ½ tsp pepper
- 1 tsp salt

Directions

1. Add sweet potatoes and Brussels sprouts in the mixing bowl.
2. Add remaining ingredients over sweet potatoes and Brussels sprouts and toss until well coated.
3. Transfer sweet potatoes and Brussels sprouts on air fryer oven tray and roast at 400 F for 10 minutes.
4. Turn sweet potatoes and Brussels sprouts to the other side and roast for 10 minutes more.
5. Serve and enjoy.

Nutrition:

Calories 138 | Fat 7.4 g | Carbohydrates 17.2 g | Sugar 3.9 g | Protein 4.4 g | Cholesterol 0 mg

21. Roasted Potato Wedges

P Prep Time 10 m | P Cooking Time 10 m | 6 Servings

Ingredients

- 2 lbs. potatoes, cut into wedges
- 2 tbsp. McCormick's chipotle seasoning
- ¼ cup olive oil

Directions

1. Add potato wedges into the mixing bowl.
2. Add remaining ingredients over potato wedges and toss until well coated.
3. Transfer potato wedges onto the air fryer oven tray roast at 400 F for 5 minutes.
4. Turn potato wedges to the other side and roast for 5 minutes more.
5. Serve and enjoy.

Nutrition

Calories 176 | Fat 8.6 g | Carbohydrates 23.8 g | Sugar 1.7 g | Protein 2.5 g | Cholesterol 0 mg

22. Breakfast Egg Bites

P Prep Time 10 m | P Cooking Time 13 m | 4 Servings

Ingredients

- 4 eggs, lightly beaten
- ¼ cup ham, diced
- ¼ cup cheddar cheese, shredded
- ¼ cup bell pepper, diced
- ½ cup milk
- Pepper
- Salt

Directions

1. Add all necessary ingredients into the mixing bowl and whisk until well combined.
2. Spray muffin silicone mold with cooking spray.
3. Pour egg mixture into the silicone muffin mold and place it in the air fryer oven and bake at 350 F for 10 minutes.
4. After 10 minutes flip egg bites and cook for 3 minutes more.
5. Serve and enjoy.

Nutrition

Calories 123 | Fat 8.1 g | Carbohydrates 2.8 g | Sugar 2.1 g | Protein 9.8 g | Cholesterol 178 mg

23. Mushroom & Pepperoncini Omelet

P Prep Time 15 m | P Cooking Time 20 m | 2 Servings

Ingredients:

- 3 large eggs
- ¼ c milk
- Salt and ground black pepper, as required
- ½ cup cheddar cheese, shredded
- ¼ cup cooked mushrooms
- 3 pepperoncini peppers, sliced thinly
- ½ tablespoon scallion, sliced thinly

Directions:

1. In a bowl, add the eggs, milk, salt and black pepper and beat well.
2. Place the mixture into a greased baking pan.
3. Press "Power Button" of Air Fry Oven and turn the dial to select the "Air Bake" mode.
4. Press the Time button and again turn the dial to set the cooking time to 20 minutes.
5. Now push the Temp button and rotate the dial to set the temperature at 350 degrees F.
6. Press "Start/Pause" button to start.
7. When the unit beeps to show that it is preheated, open the lid.
8. Arrange pan over the "Wire Rack" and insert in the oven.
9. Cut into equal-sized wedges and serve hot.

Nutrition:

Calories 254|Fat 17.5 g|Cholesterol 311 mg|Sodium 793 mg|Carbs 7.3 g|Fiber 0.1 g|Protein 8.2 g

24. Chicken Omelet

P Prep Time 10 m | P Cooking Time 16 m | 2 Servings

Ingredients:

- 1 teaspoon butter
- 1 small yellow onion, chopped
- ½ jalapeño pepper, seeded and chopped
- 3 eggs

- Salt and ground black pepper, as required
- ¼ cup cooked chicken, shredded

Directions:
1. In a frying pan, melt the butter over medium heat and cook the onion for about 4-5 minutes.
2. Add the jalapeño pepper and cook for about 1 minute.
3. Remove from the heat and set aside to cool slightly.
4. Meanwhile, in a bowl, add the eggs, salt, and black pepper and beat well.
5. Add the onion mixture and chicken and stir to combine.
6. Place the chicken mixture into a small baking pan.
7. Press "Power Button" of Air Fry Oven and turn the dial to select the "Air Fry" mode.
8. Press the Time button and again turn the dial to set the cooking time to 6 minutes.
9. Now push the Temp button and rotate the dial to set the temperature at 355 degrees F.
10. Press "Start/Pause" button to start.
11. When the unit beeps to show that it is preheated, open the lid.
12. Arrange pan over the "Wire Rack" and insert in the oven.
13. Cut the omelet into 2 portions and serve hot.

Nutrition:
Calories 153|Fat 9.1 g|Cholesterol 264 mg|Sodium 196 mg|Carbs 4 g|Fiber 0.9 g|Protein 13.8 g

25. Chicken & Zucchini Omelet

P Prep Time 15 m | P Cooking Time 35 m | 6 Servings

Ingredients:
- 8 eggs
- ½ cup milk
- Salt and ground black pepper, as required
- 1 cup cooked chicken, chopped
- 1 cup Cheddar cheese, shredded
- ½ cup fresh chives, chopped
- ¾ cup zucchini, chopped

Directions:
1. In a bowl, add the eggs, milk, salt and black pepper and beat well.
2. Add the remaining ingredients and stir to combine.
3. Place the mixture into a greased baking pan.
4. Press "Power Button" of Air Fry Oven and turn the dial to select the "Air Bake" mode.
5. Press the Time button and again turn the dial to set the cooking time to 35 minutes.
6. Now push the Temp button and rotate the dial to set the temperature at 315 degrees F.
7. Press "Start/Pause" button to start.
8. When the unit beeps to show that it is preheated, open the lid.
9. Arrange pan over the "Wire Rack" and insert in the oven.
10. Cut into equal-sized wedges and serve hot.

Nutrition:
Calories 209|Fat 13.3 g|Cholesterol 258 mg|Sodium 252 mg|Carbs 2.3 g|Fiber 0.3 g|Protein 9.8 g

26. Pepperoni Omelet

P Prep Time 15 m | P Cooking Time 12 m | 2 Servings

Ingredients:
- 4 eggs

- 2 tablespoons milk
- Pinch of salt
- Ground black pepper, as required
- 8-10 turkey pepperoni slices

Directions:
1. In a bowl, crack the eggs and beat well.
2. Add the remaining ingredients and gently, stir to combine.
3. Place the mixture into a baking pan.
4. Press "Power Button" of Air Fry Oven and turn the dial to select the "Air Fry" mode.
5. Press the Time button and again turn the dial to set the cooking time to 12 minutes.
6. Now push the Temp button and rotate the dial to set the temperature at 355 degrees F.
7. Press "Start/Pause" button to start.
8. When the unit beeps to show that it is preheated, open the lid.
9. Arrange pan over the "Wire Rack" and insert in the oven.
10. Cut into equal-sized wedges and serve hot.

Nutrition:
Calories 149|Fat 10 g|Cholesterol 337 mg|Sodium 350 mg|Carbs 1.5 g|Fiber 0 g|Protein 13.6 g

27. Sausage Omelet

P Prep Time 10 m | P Cooking Time 13 m | 2 Servings

Ingredients:
- 4 eggs
- 1 bacon slice, chopped
- 2 sausages, chopped
- 1 yellow onion, chopped

Directions:
1. In a bowl, crack the eggs and beat well.
2. Add the remaining ingredients and gently, stir to combine.
3. Place the mixture into a baking pan.
4. Press "Power Button" of Air Fry Oven and turn the dial to select the "Air Fry" mode.
5. Press the Time button and again turn the dial to set the cooking time to 13 minutes.
6. Now push the Temp button and rotate the dial to set the temperature at 320 degrees F.
7. Press "Start/Pause" button to start.
8. When the unit beeps to show that it is preheated, open the lid.
9. Arrange pan over the "Wire Rack" and insert in the oven.
10. Cut into equal-sized wedges and serve hot.

Nutrition:
Calories 325|Fat 23.1 g|Cholesterol 368 mg|Sodium 678 mg|Carbs 6 g|Fiber 1.2 g|Protein 22.7 g

28. Pancetta & Hot Dogs Omelet

P Prep Time 10 m | P Cooking Time 10 m | 2 Servings

Ingredients:
- 4 eggs
- ¼ teaspoon dried parsley
- ¼ teaspoon dried rosemary
- 1 pancetta slice, chopped
- 2 hot dogs, chopped
- 2 small onions, chopped

Directions:
1. In a bowl, crack the eggs and beat well.
2. Add the remaining ingredients and gently, stir to combine.
3. Place the mixture into a baking pan.
4. Press "Power Button" of Air Fry Oven and turn the dial to select the "Air Fry" mode.
5. Press the Time button and again turn the dial to set the cooking time to 10 minutes.
6. Now push the Temp button and rotate the dial to set the temperature at 320 degrees F.
7. Press "Start/Pause" button to start.
8. When the unit beeps to show that it is preheated, open the lid.
9. Arrange pan over the "Wire Rack" and insert in the oven.
10. Cut into equal-sized wedges and serve hot.

Nutrition:
Calories 282|Fat 19.3 g|Cholesterol 351mg|Sodium 632 mg|Carbs 8.2 g|Fiber 1.6 g|Protein 18.9 g

29. Egg & Tofu Omelet

P Prep Time 15 m | P Cooking Time 10 m | 2 Servings

Ingredients:
- 1 teaspoon arrowroot starch
- 2 teaspoons water
- 3 eggs
- 2 teaspoons fish sauce
- 1 teaspoon olive oil
- Ground black pepper, as required
- 8 oz. silken tofu, pressed and sliced

Directions:
1. In a large bowl, dissolve arrowroot starch in water.
2. Add the eggs, fish sauce, oil and black pepper and beat well.
3. Place tofu in the bottom of a greased baking pan and top with the egg mixture.
4. Press "Power Button" of Air Fry Oven and turn the dial to select the "Air Fry" mode.
5. Press the Time button and again turn the dial to set the cooking time to 10 minutes.
6. Now push the Temp button and rotate the dial to set the temperature at 390 degrees F.
7. Press "Start/Pause" button to start.
8. When the unit beeps to show that it is preheated, open the lid.
9. Arrange pan over the "Wire Rack" and insert in the oven.
10. Cut into equal-sized wedges and serve hot.

Nutrition:
Calories 192|Fat 12 g|Cholesterol 246mg|Sodium 597 mg|Carbs 4.6 g|Fiber 0.2 g|Protein 16.4 g

30. Eggs, Tofu & Mushroom Omelet

P Prep Time 15 m | P Cooking Time 35 m | 2 Servings

Ingredients:
- 2 teaspoons canola oil
- ¼ of onion, chopped
- 1 garlic clove, minced
- 8 oz. silken tofu, pressed and sliced
- 3½ oz. fresh mushrooms, sliced
- Salt and ground black pepper, as needed

- 3 eggs, beaten

Directions:
1. In a skillet, heat the oil over medium heat and sauté the onion, and garlic for about 4-5 minutes.
2. Add the mushrooms and cook for about 4-5 minutes.
3. Remove from the heat and stir in the tofu, salt and black pepper.
4. Place the tofu mixture into a pan and top with the beaten eggs.
5. Press "Power Button" of Air Fry Oven and turn the dial to select the "Air Fry" mode.
6. Press the Time button and again turn the dial to set the cooking time to 25 minutes.
7. Now push the Temp button and rotate the dial to set the temperature at 355 degrees F.
8. Press "Start/Pause" button to start.
9. When the unit beeps to show that it is preheated, open the lid.
10. Arrange pan over the "Wire Rack" and insert in the oven.
11. Cut into equal-sized wedges and serve hot.

Nutrition:
Calories 224|Fat 14.5 g|Cholesterol 246 mg|Sodium 214 mg|Carbs 6.6 g|Fiber 0.9 g|Protein 18g

31. Eggs in Bread & Bacon Cups

P Prep Time 10 m | P Cooking Time 15 m | 4 Servings

Ingredients:
4 bacon slices
4 bread slices
1 scallion, chopped
2 tablespoons bell pepper, seeded and chopped
1½ tablespoons mayonnaise
4 eggs

Directions:
1. Grease 6 cups muffin tin with cooking spray.
2. Line the sides of each prepared muffin cup with 1 bacon slice.
3. Cut bread slices with round cookie cutter.
4. Arrange the bread slice in the bottom of each muffin cup.
5. Top with, scallion, bell pepper and mayonnaise evenly.
6. Carefully, crack one egg in each muffin cup.
7. Press "Power Button" of Air Fry Oven and turn the dial to select the "Air Fry" mode.
8. Press the Time button and again turn the dial to set the cooking time to 15 minutes.
9. Now push the Temp button and rotate the dial to set the temperature at 375 degrees F.
10. Press "Start/Pause" button to start.
11. When the unit beeps to show that it is preheated, open the lid.
12. Arrange the ramekins over the "Wire Rack" and insert in the oven.
13. Serve warm.

Nutrition:
Calories 298|Fat 20.7 g|Cholesterol 197 mg|Sodium 829mg|Carbs 10.1g|Fiber 1.1g|Protein 17.6 g

32. Spinach & Mozzarella Muffins

P Prep Time 10 m | P Cooking Time 10 m | 2 Servings

Ingredients:
- 2 large eggs
- 2 tablespoons half-and-half

- 2 tablespoons frozen spinach, thawed
- 4 teaspoons mozzarella cheese, grated
- Salt and ground black pepper, as required

Directions:
1. Grease 2 ramekins.
2. In each prepared ramekin, crack 1 egg.
3. Divide the half-and-half, spinach, cheese, salt and black pepper and each ramekin and gently stir to combine, without breaking the yolks.
4. Press "Power Button" of Air Fry Oven and turn the dial to select the "Air Fry" mode.
5. Press the Time button and again turn the dial to set the cooking time to 10 minutes.
6. Now push the Temp button and rotate the dial to set the temperature at 330 degrees F.
7. Press "Start/Pause" button to start.
8. When the unit beeps to show that it is preheated, open the lid.
9. Arrange the ramekins over the "Wire Rack" and insert in the oven.
10. Serve warm.

Nutrition:
Calories 251|Fat 16.7 g|Cholesterol 222 mg|Sodium 495 mg|Carbs 3.1 g|Fiber 0 g|Protein 22.8 g

33. Bacon & Spinach Muffins

P Prep Time 10 m | P Cooking Time 17 m | 6 Servings

Ingredients:
- 6 eggs
- ½ cup milk
- Salt and ground black pepper, as required
- 1 cup fresh spinach, chopped
- 4 cooked bacon slices, crumbled

Directions:
1. In a bowl, add the eggs, milk, salt and black pepper and beat until well combined.
2. Add the spinach and stir to combine.
3. Divide the spinach mixture into 6 greased cups of an egg bite mold evenly.
4. Press "Power Button" of Air Fry Oven and turn the dial to select the "Air Fry" mode.
5. Press the Time button and again turn the dial to set the cooking time to 17 minutes.
6. Now push the Temp button and rotate the dial to set the temperature at 325 degrees F.
7. Press "Start/Pause" button to start.
8. When the unit beeps to show that it is preheated, open the lid.
9. Arrange the mold over the "Wire Rack" and insert in the oven.
10. Place the mold onto a wire rack to cool for about 5 minutes.
11. Top with bacon pieces and serve warm.

Nutrition:
Calories 179|Fat 12.9 g|Cholesterol 187 mg|Sodium 549 mg|Carbs 1.8 g|Fiber 0.1g|Protein 13.5 g

34. Ham Muffins

P Prep Time 10 m | P Cooking Time 18 m | 6 Servings

Ingredients:
- 6 ham slices
- 6 eggs
- 6 tablespoons cream

- 3 tablespoon mozzarella cheese, shredded
- ¼ teaspoon dried basil, crushed

Directions:
1. Lightly, grease 6 cups of a silicone muffin tin.
2. Line each prepared muffin cup with 1 ham slice.
3. Crack 1 egg into each muffin cup and top with cream.
4. Sprinkle with cheese and basil.
5. Press "Power Button" of Air Fry Oven and turn the dial to select the "Air Fry" mode.
6. Press the Time button and again turn the dial to set the cooking time to 18 minutes.
7. Now push the Temp button and rotate the dial to set the temperature at 350 degrees F.
8. Press "Start/Pause" button to start.
9. When the unit beeps to show that it is preheated, open the lid.
10. Arrange the muffin tin over the "Wire Rack" and insert in the oven.
11. Place the muffin tin onto a wire rack to cool for about 5 minutes.
12. Carefully, invert the muffins onto the platter and serve warm.

Nutrition:
Calories 156|Fat 10 g|Cholesterol 189 mg|Sodium 516 mg|Carbs 2.3 g|Fiber 0.4g|Protein 14.3 g

35. Savory Carrot Muffins

P Prep Time 15 m | P Cooking Time 7 m | 6 Servings

Ingredients:
- For Muffins:
- ¼ cup whole-wheat flour
- ¼ cup all-purpose flour
- ½ teaspoon baking powder
- 1/8 teaspoon baking soda
- ½ teaspoon dried parsley, crushed
- ½ teaspoon salt
- ½ cup plain yogurt
- 1 teaspoon vinegar
- 1 tablespoon vegetable oil
- 3 tablespoons cottage cheese, grated
- 1 carrot, peeled and grated
- 2-4 tablespoons water (if needed)
- For Topping:
- 7 oz. Parmesan cheese, grated
- ¼ cup walnuts, chopped

Directions:
1. For muffin: in a large bowl, mix together the flours, baking powder, baking soda, parsley, and salt.
2. In another large bowl, mix well the yogurt, and vinegar.
3. Add the remaining ingredients except water and beat them well. (add some water if needed)
4. Make a well in the center of the yogurt mixture.
5. Slowly, add the flour mixture in the well and mix until well combined.
6. Place the mixture into lightly greased muffin molds evenly and top with the Parmesan cheese and walnuts.
7. Press "Power Button" of Air Fry Oven and turn the dial to select the "Air Fry" mode.

8. Press the Time button and again turn the dial to set the cooking time to 7 minutes.
9. Now push the Temp button and rotate the dial to set the temperature at 355 degrees F.
10. Press "Start/Pause" button to start.
11. When the unit beeps to show that it is preheated, open the lid.
12. Arrange the ramekins over "Wire Rack" and insert in the oven.
13. Place the muffin molds onto a wire rack to cool for about 5 minutes.
14. Carefully, invert the muffins onto the platter and serve warm.

Nutrition:
Calories 292|Fat 13.1 g|Cholesterol 25 mg|Sodium 579 mg|Carbs 27.2 g|Fiber 1.5g|Protein 17.7 g

Beef, Lamb & Pork Recipes

36. Saucy beef bake

P Prep Time 10 m | P Cooking Time 36 m | 6 Servings

Ingredients

- tablespoons olive oil
- 1 large onion, diced
- lbs. (907.185g) Ground beef
- teaspoons salt
- cloves garlic, chopped
- 1/2 cup red wine
- cloves garlic, chopped
- teaspoons ground cinnamon
- teaspoons ground cumin
- teaspoons dried oregano
- 1 teaspoon black pepper
- 1 can 28 oz. Crushed tomatoes
- 1 tablespoon tomato paste

Directions:

1 Put a suitable wok over moderate heat and add oil to heat.
2 Toss in onion, salt, and beef meat then stir cook for 12 minutes.
3 Stir in red wine and cook for 2 minutes.
4 Add cinnamon, garlic, oregano, cumin, and pepper, then stir cook for 2 minutes.
5 Add tomato paste and tomatoes and cook for 20 minutes on a simmer.
6 Spread this mixture in a casserole dish.
7 Press "power button" of air fry oven and turn the dial to select the "bake" mode.
8 Press the time button and again turn the dial to set the cooking time to 30 minutes.
9 Now push the temp button and rotate the dial to set the temperature at 350 degrees f.
10 Once preheated, place casserole dish in the oven and close its lid.
11 Serve warm.

Nutrition:

Calories 405|Fat 22.7 g|Cholesterol 4 mg|Sodium 227 mg|Carbs 26.1 g|Fiber 1.4 g|Protein 45.2 g

37. Parmesan meatballs

P Prep Time 10 m | P Cooking Time 20 m | 6 Servings

Ingredients

- lbs. (907.185g) Ground beef
- eggs
- 1 cup ricotta cheese
- 1/4 cup parmesan cheese shredded
- 1/2 cup panko breadcrumbs
- 1/4 cup basil chopped
- 1/4 cup parsley chopped
- 1 tablespoon fresh oregano chopped
- teaspoon kosher salt
- 1 teaspoon ground fennel
- 1/2 teaspoon red pepper flakes

- 32 oz. spaghetti sauce, to serve

Directions:

1 Thoroughly mix the beef with all other ingredients for meatballs in a bowl.
2 Make small meatballs out of this mixture then place them in the air fryer basket.
3 Press "power button" of air fry oven and turn the dial to select the "bake" mode.
4 Press the time button and again turn the dial to set the cooking time to 20 minutes.
5 Now push the temp button and rotate the dial to set the temperature at 400 degrees f.
6 Once preheated, place meatballs basket in the oven and close its lid.
7 Flip the meatballs when cooked halfway through then resume cooking.
8 Pour spaghetti sauce on top.
9 Serve warm.

Nutrition:

Calories 545| Total fat 36.4 g |Saturated fat 10.1 g| Protein 42.5 g

38. Tricolor beef skewers

P Prep Time 10 m | P Cooking Time 25 m | 4 Servings

Ingredients

- garlic cloves, minced
- tablespoon rapeseed oil
- 1 cup cottage cheese, cubed
- cherry tomatoes
- tablespoon cider vinegar
- Large bunch thyme
- 1 ¼ lb. (566.99g) Boneless beef, diced

Directions:

1. Toss beef with all its thyme, oil, vinegar, and garlic.
2. Marinate the thyme beef for 2 hours in a closed container in the refrigerator.
3. Thread the marinated beef, cheese, and tomatoes on the skewers.
4. Place these skewers in an air fryer basket.
5. Press "power button" of air fry oven and turn the dial to select the "air fry" mode.
6. Press the time button and again turn the dial to set the cooking time to 25 minutes.
7. Now push the temp button and rotate the dial to set the temperature at 350 degrees f.
8. Once preheated, place the air fryer basket in the oven and close its lid.
9. Flip the skewers when cooked halfway through then resume cooking.
10. Serve warm.

Nutrition:

Calories 695 |Total fat 17.5 g |Saturated fat 4.8 g |Protein 117.4 g

39. Yogurt beef kebabs

P Prep Time 10 m | P Cooking Time 25 m | 4 Servings

Ingredients

- ½ cup yogurt
- 1½ tablespoon mint
- 1 teaspoon ground cumin
- 1 cup eggplant, diced
- oz. Lean beef, diced
- ½ small onion, cubed

Directions:

1 Whisk yogurt with mint and cumin in a suitable bowl.
2 Toss in beef cubes and mix well to coat. Marinate for 30 minutes.
3 Alternatively, thread the beef, onion, and eggplant on the skewers.
4 Place these beef skewers in the air fry basket.
5 Press "power button" of air fry oven and turn the dial to select the "air fryer" mode.
6 Press the time button and again turn the dial to set the cooking time to 25 minutes.
7 Now push the temp button and rotate the dial to set the temperature at 370 degrees f.
8 Once preheated, place the air fryer basket in the oven and close its lid.
9 Flip the skewers when cooked halfway through then resume cooking.
10 Serve warm.

Nutrition:
Calories 301 |Total fat 8.9 g| Saturated fat 4.5 g | Protein 15.3 g

40. Agave beef kebabs

P Prep Time 10 m | P Cooking Time 20 m | 6 Servings

Ingredients
- lbs. (907.185g) Beef steaks, cubed
- tablespoon jerk seasoning
- Zest and juice of 1 lime
- 1 tablespoon agave syrup
- ½ teaspoon thyme leaves, chopped

Directions:
1 Mix beef with jerk seasoning, lime juice, zest, agave and thyme.
2 Toss well to coat then marinate for 30 minutes.
3 Alternatively, thread the beef on the skewers.
4 Place these beef skewers in the air fry basket.
5 Press "power button" of air fry oven and turn the dial to select the "air fryer" mode.
6 Press the time button and again turn the dial to set the cooking time to 20 minutes.
7 Now push the temp button and rotate the dial to set the temperature at 360 degrees f.
8 Once preheated, place the air fryer basket in the oven and close its lid.
9 Flip the skewers when cooked halfway through then resume cooking.
10 Serve warm.

Nutrition:
Calories 548|Fat 22.9 g|Cholesterol 105 mg|Sodium 350mg|Carbs 17.5g|Fiber 6.3g|Protein 40.1 g

41. Beef skewers with potato salad

P Prep Time 10 m | P Cooking Time 25 m | 4 Servings

Ingredients
- Juice ½ lemon
- tablespoon olive oil
- 1 garlic clove, crushed
- 1 ¼ lb. (566.99g) Diced beef
- For the salad
- potatoes, boiled, peeled and diced
- large tomatoes, chopped
- 1 cucumber, chopped
- 1 handful black olives, chopped

- oz. Pack feta cheese, crumbled
- 1 bunch of mint, chopped

Directions:

1 Whisk lemon juice with garlic and olive oil in a bowl.
2 Toss in beef cubes and mix well to coat. Marinate for 30 minutes.
3 Alternatively, thread the beef on the skewers.
4 Place these beef skewers in the air fry basket.
5 Press "power button" of air fry oven and turn the dial to select the "air fryer" mode.
6 Press the time button and again turn the dial to set the cooking time to 25 minutes.
7 Now push the temp button and rotate the dial to set the temperature at 360 degrees f.
8 Once preheated, place the air fryer basket in the oven and close its lid.
9 Flip the skewers when cooked halfway through then resume cooking.
10 Meanwhile, whisk all the salad ingredients in a salad bowl.
11 Serve the skewers with prepared salad.

Nutrition:

Calories 609|Fat 50.5 g|Cholesterol 58 mg|Sodium 463 mg|Carbs 9.9 g|Fiber 1.5 g|Protein 29.3 g

42. Classic souvlaki kebobs

P Prep Time 10 m | P Cooking Time 20 m | 6 Servings

Ingredients

- lbs. (907.185g) Beef shoulder fat trimmed, cut into chunks
- 1/3 cup olive oil
- ½ cup red wine
- teaspoon dried oregano
- ½ cup of orange juice
- 1 teaspoon orange zest
- garlic cloves, crushed

Directions:

1 Whisk olive oil, red wine, oregano, oranges juice, zest, and garlic in a suitable bowl.
2 Toss in beef cubes and mix well to coat. Marinate for 30 minutes.
3 Alternatively, thread the beef, onion, and bread on the skewers.
4 Place these beef skewers in the air fry basket.
5 Press "power button" of air fry oven and turn the dial to select the "air fryer" mode.
6 Press the time button and again turn the dial to set the cooking time to 20 minutes.
7 Now push the temp button and rotate the dial to set the temperature at 370 degrees f.
8 Once preheated, place the air fryer basket in the oven and close its lid.
9 Flip the skewers when cooked halfway through then resume cooking.
10 Serve warm.

Nutrition:

Calories 537|Fat 19.8 g|Cholesterol 10 mg|Sodium 719 mg|Carbs 25.1 g|Fiber 0.9g|Protein 37.8 g

43. Harissa dipped beef skewers

P Prep Time 10 m | P Cooking Time 16 m | 6 Servings

Ingredients

- 1 lb. (453.592g) Beef mince
- tablespoon harissa
- oz. Feta cheese

- 1 large red onion, shredded
- 1 handful parsley, chopped
- 1 handful mint, chopped
- 1 tablespoon olive oil
- Juice 1 lemon

Directions:

1 Whisk beef mince with harissa, onion, feta, and seasoning in a bowl.
2 Make 12 sausages out of this mixture then thread them on the skewers.
3 Place these beef skewers in the air fry basket.
4 Press "power button" of air fry oven and turn the dial to select the "bake" mode.
5 Press the time button and again turn the dial to set the cooking time to 16 minutes.
6 Now push the temp button and rotate the dial to set the temperature at 370 degrees f.
7 Once preheated, place the air fryer basket in the oven and close its lid.
8 Flip the skewers when cooked halfway through then resume cooking.
9 Toss the remaining salad ingredients in a salad bowl.
10 Serve beef skewers with tomato salad.

Nutrition:

Calories 452 |Total fat 4 g| Saturated fat 2 g | Cholesterol 65 mg

44. Onion pepper beef kebobs

P Prep Time 10 m | P Cooking Time 20 m | 4 Servings

Ingredients

- tablespoon pesto paste
- 2/3 lb. (303.9g) Beefsteak, diced
- red peppers, cut into chunks
- red onions, cut into wedges
- 1 tablespoon olive oil

Directions:

1 Toss in beef cubes with harissa and oil, then mix well to coat. Marinate for 30 minutes.
2 Alternatively, thread the beef, onion, and peppers on the skewers.
3 Place these beef skewers in the air fry basket.
4 Press "power button" of air fry oven and turn the dial to select the "air fryer" mode.
5 Press the time button and again turn the dial to set the cooking time to 20 minutes.
6 Now push the temp button and rotate the dial to set the temperature at 370 degrees f.
7 Once preheated, place the air fryer basket in the oven and close its lid.
8 Flip the skewers when cooked halfway through then resume cooking.
9 Serve warm.

Nutrition:

Calories 301 |Total fat 15.8 g |Saturated fat 2.7 g |Cholesterol 75 mg

45. Mayo spiced kebobs

P Prep Time 10 m | P Cooking Time 10 m | 4 Servings

Ingredients

- tablespoon cumin seed
- tablespoon coriander seed
- tablespoon fennel seed
- 1 tablespoon paprika
- tablespoon garlic mayonnaise

- garlic cloves, finely minced
- ½ teaspoon ground cinnamon
- 1 ½ lb. (680.389g) Lean minced beef

Directions:
1 Blend all the spices and seeds with garlic, cream, and cinnamon in a blender.
2 Add this cream paste to the minced beef then mix well.
3 Make 8 sausages and thread each on the skewers.
4 Place these beef skewers in the air fry basket.
5 Press "power button" of air fry oven and turn the dial to select the "air fryer" mode.
6 Press the time button and again turn the dial to set the cooking time to 10 minutes.
7 Now push the temp button and rotate the dial to set the temperature at 370 degrees f.
8 Once preheated, place the air fryer basket in the oven and close its lid.
9 Flip the skewers when cooked halfway through then resume cooking.
10 Serve warm.

Nutrition:
Calories 308| Total fat 20.5 g| Saturated fat 3 g | Cholesterol 42 mg

46. Beef with orzo salad

P Prep Time 10 m | P Cooking Time 27 m | 4 Servings

Ingredients
- 2/3 lbs. Beef shoulder, cubed
- 1 teaspoon ground cumin
- ½ teaspoon cayenne pepper
- 1 teaspoon sweet smoked paprika
- 1 tablespoon olive oil
- 24 cherry tomatoes
- Salad:
- ½ cup orzo, boiled
- ½ cup frozen pea
- 1 large carrot, grated
- Small pack coriander, chopped
- Small pack mint, chopped
- Juice 1 lemon
- tablespoon olive oil

Directions:
1 Toss tomatoes and beef with oil, paprika, pepper, and cumin in a bowl.
2 Alternatively, thread the beef and tomatoes on the skewers.
3 Place these beef skewers in the air fry basket.
4 Press "power button" of air fry oven and turn the dial to select the "air fryer" mode.
5 Press the time button and again turn the dial to set the cooking time to 25 minutes.
6 Now push the temp button and rotate the dial to set the temperature at 370 degrees f.
7 Once preheated, place the air fryer basket in the oven and close its lid.
8 Flip the skewers when cooked halfway through then resume cooking.
9 Meanwhile, sauté carrots and peas with olive oil in a pan for 2 minutes.
10 Stir in mint, lemon juice, coriander, and cooked couscous.

Nutrition:
Calories 231|Fat 20.1 g|Cholesterol 110 mg|Sodium 941mg|Carbs 20.1g|Fiber 0.9g|Protein 14.6 g

47. Beef zucchini shashliks

P Prep Time 10 m | P Cooking Time 25 m | 4 Servings

Ingredients

- 1lb. (453.592g) Beef, boned and diced
- 1 lime, juiced and chopped
- tablespoon olive oil
- 20 garlic cloves, chopped
- 1 handful rosemary, chopped
- green peppers, cubed
- zucchinis, cubed
- red onions, cut into wedges

Directions:

1 Toss the beef with the rest of the skewer's ingredients in a bowl.
2 Thread the beef, peppers, zucchini, and onion on the skewers.
3 Place these beef skewers in the air fry basket.
4 Press "power button" of air fry oven and turn the dial to select the "air fryer" mode.
5 Press the time button and again turn the dial to set the cooking time to 25 minutes.
6 Now push the temp button and rotate the dial to set the temperature at 370 degrees f.
7 Once preheated, place the air fryer basket in the oven and close its lid.
8 Flip the skewers when cooked halfway through then resume cooking.
9 Serve warm.

Nutrition:

Calories 472|Fat 11.1 g|Cholesterol 610mg|Sodium 749 mg|Carbs 19.9g|Fiber 0.2g|Protein 13.5 g

48. Spiced beef skewers

P Prep Time 10 m | P Cooking Time 18 m | 4 Servings

Ingredients

- teaspoons ground cumin
- teaspoons ground coriander
- 1/4 teaspoon ground cinnamon
- 1/8 teaspoon ground smoked paprika
- teaspoons lime zest
- 1/2 teaspoon salt
- 1/2 teaspoon black pepper
- 1 tablespoon lemon juice
- teaspoons olive oil
- 1 1/2 lbs. Lean beef, cubed

Directions:

1 Toss beef with the rest of the skewer's ingredients in a bowl.
2 Thread the beef and veggies on the skewers alternately.
3 Place these beef skewers in the air fry basket.
4 Press "power button" of air fry oven and turn the dial to select the "air fryer" mode.
5 Press the time button and again turn the dial to set the cooking time to 18 minutes.
6 Now push the temp button and rotate the dial to set the temperature at 370 degrees f.
7 Once preheated, place the air fryer basket in the oven and close its lid.
8 Flip the skewers when cooked halfway through then resume cooking.
9 Serve warm.

Nutrition:
Calories 327|Fat 3.5 g|Cholesterol 162 mg|Sodium 142 mg|Carbs 33.6 g|Protein 24.5 g

49. Cheeseburger Egg Rolls

P Prep Time 10 m | P Cooking Time 7 m | 6 Servings

Ingredients
- 6 egg roll wrappers
- 6 chopped dill pickle chips
- 1 tbsp. yellow mustard
- 3 tbsp. cream cheese
- 3 tbsp. shredded cheddar cheese
- ½ C. chopped onion
- ½ C. chopped bell pepper
- ¼ tsp. onion powder
- ¼ tsp. garlic powder
- 8 ounces of raw lean ground beef

Directions
1.   In a skillet, add the spices, meat, onion, and bell pepper. Stir and mash the meat until it is fully cooked and the vegetables are soft.
2.   Remove skillet from heat and add cream cheese, mustard, and cheddar cheese, stirring until melted.
3.   Pour the meat mixture into a bowl and add the pickles.
4.   Place egg wrappers and spoon 1/6 of the meat mixture into each. Dampen the edges of the egg roll with water. Fold the sides in half and seal with water.
5.   Repeat with all the other egg rolls.
6.   Place the rolls in a deep fryer, one batch at a time.
7.   Pour into the Oven rack/basket. Place the air fryer Rack on the middle-shelf of the Smart Air Fryer Oven. Set temperature to 391°F, and set time to 7 minutes.

Nutrition
Calories 153 |Fat 4 g |Protein 12 g |Sugar 3 g

50. Air Fried Grilled Steak

P Prep Time 5 m | P Cooking Time 45 m | 2 Servings

Ingredients
- Top sirloin steaks
- Tablespoons butter, melted
- 3 tablespoons olive oil
- Salt and pepper to taste

Directions
1.   Preheat the Smart Air Fryer for 5 minutes.
2.   Season the sirloin steaks with olive oil, salt, and pepper.
3.   Place the beef in the air fryer oven basket.
4.   Cook for 45 minutes at 350°F.
5.   Once cooked, serve with butter.

Nutrition
Calories 1536 |Fat 123.7 g |Protein 103.4 g

51. Juicy Cheeseburgers

P Prep Time 5 m | P Cooking Time 15 m | 4 Servings

Ingredients

- 1 pound 93% lean ground beef
- 1 teaspoon Worcestershire sauce
- 1 tablespoon burger seasoning
- Salt
- Pepper
- Cooking oil
- Slices cheese
- Buns

Directions

1. In a large bowl, combine the ground beef, Worcestershire, hamburger seasoning, and salt and pepper to taste until well combined. Spray the fryer basket with cooking oil. You will only need a quick spray because hamburgers produce oil while they cook. Form 4 patties with the mixture. Place the burgers in the deep fryer. Burgers should fit without having to be stacked, but stacking is fine if necessary.
2. Place on the oven rack/basket. Place the rack on the middle shelf of the Smart Air Fryer. Set the temperature to 375 ° F and set the time to 8 minutes. Cook for 8 minutes. Open the fryer and flip the patties—Cook for 3 to 4 more minutes. Check the inside of the patties to see if they have finished cooking. You can stick a knife or fork in the center to examine the color.
3. Fill each burger with a slice of cheese. Cook for one more minute or until cheese is melted. Serve on buns with any additional toppings of your choice.

Nutrition

Calories 566 |Fat 39 g |Protein 29 g |Fiber 1 g

52. Spicy Thai Beef Stir-Fry

P Prep Time 15 m | P Cooking Time 9 m | 4 Servings

Ingredients

- 1 pound sirloin steaks, thinly sliced
- Tablespoons lime juice, divided
- ⅓ cup crunchy peanut butter
- ½ cup beef broth
- 1 tablespoon olive oil
- 1½ cups broccoli florets
- Cloves garlic, sliced
- 1 to 2 red chile peppers, sliced

Directions

1. In a medium bowl, combine the steak with 1 tablespoon of the lime juice. Set aside.
2. Combine the peanut butter and beef broth in a small bowl and mix well. Drain the beef and add the juice from the bowl into the peanut butter mixture.
3. In a 6-inch metal bowl, combine the olive oil, steak, and broccoli.
4. Pour into the Oven rack/basket. Place the air fryer Rack on the middle-shelf of the Smart Air Fryer Oven. Set temperature to 375°F, and set time to 4 minutes. Cook for 4 more minutes or until the steak is almost cooked and the broccoli is crisp and tender, shaking the basket once during cooking time.
5. Add the garlic, chile peppers, and the peanut butter mixture and stir.
6. Cook for 5 more minutes or until the sauce is bubbling and the broccoli is tender.
7. Serve over hot rice.

Nutrition
Calories 387 | Fat 22 g |Protein 42 g |Fiber 2 g

53. Beef Brisket Recipe from Texas

P Prep Time 15 m | P Cooking Time 1 h 30 m | 8 Servings

Ingredients
- 1 ½ cup beef stock
- 1 bay leaf
- 1 tablespoon garlic powder
- 1 tablespoon onion powder
- Pounds beef brisket, trimmed
- 2 tablespoons chili powder
- 2 teaspoons dry mustard
- Tablespoons olive oil
- Salt and pepper to taste

Directions
1. Preheat the Air Fryer Oven for 5 minutes. Place all ingredients in a deep baking dish that will fit in the air fryer.
2. Bake for 1 hour and 30 minutes at 400°F.
3. Stir the beef every after 30 minutes to soak in the sauce.

Nutrition
Calories 306 |Fat 24.1 g |Protein 18.3 g

54. Copycat Taco Bell Crunch Wraps

P Prep Time 10 m | P Cooking Time 2 m | 6 Servings

Ingredients
- Wheat tostadas
- C. sour cream
- 2 C. Mexican blend cheese
- 2 C. shredded lettuce
- 12 ounces low-sodium nacho cheese
- Roma tomatoes
- 12-inch wheat tortillas
- 1 1/3 C. water
- 2 packets low-sodium taco seasoning
- 2 pounds of lean ground beef

Directions
1. Ensure your air fryer is preheated to 400 degrees.
2. Make beef according to taco seasoning packets.
3. Place 2/3 C. prepared beef, 4 tbsp. cheese, 1 tostada, 1/3 C. sour cream, 1/3 C. lettuce, 1/6th of tomatoes, and 1/3 C. cheese on each tortilla.
4. Fold up tortillas edges and repeat with remaining ingredients. Lay the folded sides of tortillas down into the air fryer and spray with olive oil.
5. Set temperature to 400°F, and set time to 2 minutes. Cook 2 minutes until browned.

Nutrition
Calories 311 |Fat 9g |Protein 22g |Sugar 2g

55. Steak and Mushroom Gravy

P Prep Time 15 m | P Cooking Time 15 m | 4 Servings

Ingredients

- Cubed steaks
- 2 large eggs
- 1/2 dozen mushrooms
- Tablespoons unsalted butter
- Tablespoons black pepper
- 2 tablespoons salt
- 1/2 teaspoon onion powder
- 1/2 teaspoon garlic powder
- 1/4 teaspoon cayenne powder
- 1 1/4 teaspoons paprika
- 1 1/2 cups whole milk
- 1/3 cup flour
- Tablespoons vegetable oil

Directions

1. Mix 1/2 flour and a pinch of black pepper in a shallow bowl or on a plate.
2. Beat 2 eggs in a bowl and mix with a pinch of salt and pepper.
3. In another shallow bowl, mix the other half of the flour with pepper to taste, garlic powder, paprika, cayenne, and onion powder.
4. Chop the mushrooms and reserve.
5. Squeeze the fillet into the first bowl of flour, then dip it into the egg and then press the fillet into the second bowl of flour until completely covered.
6. Place on the oven rack/basket. Place the rack on the middle shelf of the Smart Air Fryer. Set the temperature to 360 ° F and set the time to 15 minutes by turning it halfway.
7. While the steak is cooking, heat the butter over medium heat and add the mushrooms to the stir-fry.
8. Add 4 tablespoons of flour and pepper to the skillet and mix until there are no lumps of flour.
9. Mix in whole milk and simmer.

Nutrition

Calories 442 |Fat 27 g |Protein 32 g |Fiber 2.3 g

56. Air Fryer Beef Casserole

P Prep Time 5 m | P Cooking Time 30 m | 4 Servings

Ingredients

- 1 green bell pepper, seeded and chopped
- 1 onion, chopped
- 1-pound ground beef
- Cloves of garlic, minced
- Tablespoons olive oil
- Cups eggs, beaten
- Salt and pepper to taste

Directions

1. Preheat the Smart Air Fryer oven for 5 minutes.
2. In a skillet that will fit in the deep fryer, combine the ground beef, onion, garlic, olive oil, and pepper. Season with salt and pepper to taste.
3. Add the beaten eggs and mix well.

4.   Place the plate with the meat and egg mixture in the deep fryer.

5.   Place on the oven rack/basket. Place the rack on the middle shelf of the Smart Air Fryer. Set the temperature to 325 ° F and set the time to 30 minutes. Bake for 30 minutes.

Nutrition

Calories 1520 |Fat 125.11 g |Protein 87.9 g

57. Asian Inspired Sichuan Lamb

P Prep Time 5 m | P Cooking Time 10 m | 4 Servings

Ingredients:

- 1 ½ tablespoons cumin seed (do not use ground cumin)
- 1 teaspoon Sichuan peppers or ½ teaspoon cayenne
- 2 tablespoons vegetable oil
- 1 tablespoon garlic, peeled and minced
- 1 tablespoon light soy sauce
- 2 red chili peppers, seeded and chopped (use gloves)
- ¼ teaspoon granulated sugar
- ½ teaspoon salt
- 1 pound lamb shoulder, cut in ½ to 1-inch pieces
- 2 green onions, chopped
- 1 handful fresh cilantro, chopped

Directions:

1.   Turn on the burner to medium high on the stove and heat up a dry skillet. Pour in the cumin seed and Sichuan peppers or cayenne and toast until fragrant. Turn off the burner and set aside until they are cool. Grind them in a grinder or mortar and pestle.

2.   In a large bowl that will contain the marinade and the lamb, combine the vegetable oil, garlic, soy sauce, chili peppers, granulated sugar and salt. Pour in the cumin/pepper combination and mix well.

3.   Using a fork, poke holes in the lamb all over the top and bottom. Place the lamb in the marinade, cover and refrigerate. You can also use a closeable plastic bag.

4.   Preheat the air fryer to 360 degrees for 5 minutes.

5.   Spray the basket with cooking spray.

6.   Remove the lamb pieces from the marinade with tongs or slotted spoon and place in basket of the air fryer in a single layer. You may need to do more than 1 batch.

7.   Cook for 10 minutes, flipping over 1 half way through. Make sure the lamb's internal temperature is 145 degrees F with a meat thermometer. Put on a serving platter and repeat with rest of the lamb.

8.   Sprinkle the chopped green onions and cilantro over top, stir and serve.

Nutrition:

Calories: 142| Fat: 7g |Protein: 17g| Fiber: 4g

58. Garlic and Rosemary Lamb Cutlets

P Prep Time 30 m | P Cooking Time 25 m | 2 Servings

Ingredients:

- 2 lamb racks (with 3 cutlets per rack)
- 2 cloves garlic, peeled and thinly sliced into slivers
- 2 long sprigs of fresh rosemary, leaves removed
- 2 tablespoon wholegrain mustard
- 1 tablespoon honey

- 2 tablespoons mint sauce (I use mint jelly)

Directions:

1. Trim fat from racks and cut slits with a sharp knife in the top of the lamb. Insert slices of the garlic and rosemary leaves in the slits and set the lamb aside.
2. Make the marinade by whisking the mustard, honey and mint sauce together and brush over the lamb racks. Let marinade in a cool area for 20 minutes.
3. Preheat the air fryer to 360 degrees for about 5 minutes.
4. Spray the basket using cooking spray and place the lamb rack or racks into the basket, propping them up however you can get them in to fit.
5. Cook 10 minutes, open and turn the racks and cook 10 more minutes.
6. Place on a platter and cover with foil to let sit 10 minutes before slicing and serving.

Nutrition:

Calories: 309| Fat: 2g |Protein: 33g| Fiber: 16g

59. Garlic Sauced Lamb Chops

P Prep Time 15 m | P Cooking Time 25 m | 4 Servings

Ingredients:

- 1 garlic bulb
- 1 teaspoon + 3 tablespoons olive oil
- 1 tablespoon fresh oregano, chopped fine
- ¼ teaspoon ground pepper
- ½ teaspoon sea salt
- 8 lamb chops

Directions:

1. Preheat the air fryer to 400 degrees F 5 minutes and while it is preheating take excess paper from the garlic bulb.
2. Coat the garlic bulb with the 1 teaspoon of olive oil and drop it in the basket that has treated with cooking spray. Roast for 12 minutes.
3. Combine the 3 tablespoons of olive oil, oregano, salt and pepper and lightly coat the lamb chops on both with the resulting oil. Let them sit at room temperature for 5 minutes.
4. Remove the garlic bulb from the basket and if it is cool, preheat again to 400 degrees for 3 minutes.
5. Spray the air fryer basket with cooking oil and place 4 chops in cooking at 400 degrees F for 5 minutes. Place them on a platter and cover to keep them warm while you do the other chops.
6. Squeeze each garlic clove between the thumb and index finger into a small bowl.
7. Taste and add salt and pepper and mix. Serve along the chops like serving ketchup.

Nutrition:

Calories: 194| Fat: 11g| Protein: 29g| Fiber: 13g

60. Herb Encrusted Lamb Chops

P Prep Time 5 m | P Cooking Time 15 m | 2 Servings

Ingredients:

- 1 teaspoon oregano
- 1 teaspoon coriander
- 1 teaspoon thyme
- 1 teaspoon rosemary
- ½ teaspoon salt

- ¼ teaspoon pepper
- 2 tablespoons lemon juice
- 2 tablespoons olive oil
- 1 pound lamb chops

Directions:

1. In a closeable bag, combine the oregano, coriander, thyme, rosemary, salt, pepper, lemon juice and olive oil and shake well so it mixes.
2. Place the chops in the bag and squish around so the mixture is on them. Refrigerate 1 hour.
3. Preheat the air fryer to 390 degrees F for 5 minutes.
4. Place the chops in the basket that has been sprayed with cooking spray.
5. Cook for 3 minutes and pause. Flip the chops to the other side and cook for another 4 minutes for medium rare. If you want them better done cook 4 minutes, pause, turn and cook 5 more minutes.

Nutrition:
Calories: 321|Fat: 34g| Protein: 18g |Fiber: 15g

61. Herbed Rack of Lamb

P Prep Time 15 m | P Cooking Time 35 m | 2 Servings

Ingredients:

- 1 tablespoon olive oil
- 1 clove garlic, peeled and minced
- 1 ½ teaspoons fresh ground pepper
- 1 tablespoon fresh rosemary, chopped
- 1 tablespoon fresh thyme, chopped
- ¾ cup breadcrumbs
- 1 egg
- 1 to 2 pound rack of lamb

Directions:

1. Place the olive oil in a small dish and add the garlic. Mix well.
2. Brush the garlic on the rack of lamb and season with pepper.
3. In one bowl combine the rosemary, thyme and breadcrumbs and break the egg and whisk in another bowl.
4. Preheat air fryer 350 degrees F for 5 minutes. Spray with cooking spray.
5. Dip the rack in the egg and then place in the breadcrumb mixture and coat the rack.
6. Place rack in air fryer basket and cook 20 minutes.
7. Raise the temperature to 400 degrees F and set for 5 more minutes.
8. Tear a piece of aluminum foil that will fit to wrap the rack. Take it out of the basket with tongs and put it in the middle of the foil. Carefully wrap and let sit about 10 minutes. Unwrap and serve.

Nutrition:
Calories: 282 |Fat: 23g |Protein: 26g| Fiber: 23g

62. Lamb Roast with Root Vegetables

P Prep Time 35 m | P Cooking Time 1 h 15 m | 6 Servings

Ingredients:

- 4 cloves garlic, peeled and sliced thin, divided
- 2 springs fresh rosemary, leaves pulled off, divided

- 3 pound leg of lamb
- Salt and pepper to taste, divided
- 2 medium sized sweet potatoes, peeled and cut into wedges
- 2 tablespoon oil, divided
- 2 cups baby carrots
- 1 teaspoon butter
- 4 large red potatoes, cubed

Directions:

1.   Slice the garlic and take the leaves of the rosemary.
2.   Cut about 5 to 6 slits in the top of the lamb and insert slices of garlic and some rosemary in each. Salt and pepper the roast to your taste and set aside to cook after the vegetables are done.
3.   Coat the sweet potatoes in 1 tablespoon of olive oil and season with salt and pepper.
4.   Spray the basket of the air fryer with cooking spray and put in the wedges. You may have to do two batches. Set for 400 degrees F and air fry 8 minutes, shake and cook another 8 minutes or so. Dump into a bowl and cover with foil.
5.   Place the carrots in some foil to cover and put the butter on top of them. Enclose them in the foil and place them in the air fryer. Set for 400 degrees for 20 minutes. Remove from the air fryer.
6.   Coat the basket with cooking spray. Mix the red potatoes with the other tablespoon of oil and salt and pepper to taste. Place in the air fryer oven and cook at 400 degrees F for 20 minutes, shaking after 10 minutes have elapsed.
7.   Use a foil tray or baking dish that fits into the air fryer and coat with cooking spray. Place the left over garlic and rosemary in the bottom and place the lamb on top.
8.   Set for 380 degrees F and cook 1 hour, checking after 30 minutes and 45 minutes to make sure it isn't getting too done. Increase the air fryer oven heat to 400 degrees F and cook for 10 to 15 minutes.
9.   Remove the roast from the air fryer and set on a platter. Cover with foil and rest 10 minutes while you dump all the vegetables back in the basket and cooking at 350 degrees F for 8 to 10 minutes or until heated through.
10.   Serve all together.

Nutrition:
Calories: 398| Fat: 5g |Protein: 18g| Fiber: 30.3g

63. Lemon and Cumin Coated Rack of Lamb

P Prep Time 15 m | P Cooking Time 200 m | 4 Servings

Ingredients:

- 1 ½ to 1 ¾ pound Frenched rack of lamb
- Salt and pepper to taste
- ½ cup breadcrumbs
- 1 teaspoon cumin seed
- 1 teaspoon ground cumin
- ½ teaspoon salt
- 1 teaspoon garlic, peeled and grated
- Lemon zest (1/4 of a lemon)
- 1 teaspoon vegetable or olive oil
- 1 egg, beaten

Directions:

1. Season the lamb rack with pepper and salt to taste and set it aside.
2. In a large bowl, combine the breadcrumbs, cumin seed, ground cumin, salt, garlic, lemon zest and oil and set aside.
3. In another bowl, beat the egg.
4. Preheat to air fryer to 250 degrees F for 5 minutes
5. Dip the rack in the egg to coat and then into the breadcrumb mixture. Make sure it is well coated.
6. Spray the basket of the air fryer using cooking spray and put the rack in. You may have to bend it a little to get it to fit.
7. Set for 250 degrees and cook 25 minutes.
8. Increase temperature to 400 degrees F and cook another 5 minutes. Check internal temperature to make sure it is 145 degrees for medium rare or more.
9. Remove rack when done and cover with foil for 10 minutes before separating ribs into individual servings.

Nutrition:
Calories: 276 |Fat: 24g| Protein: 33g |Fiber: 12.3g

64. Macadamia Rack of Lamb

P Prep Time 20 m | P Cooking Time 32 m | 4 Servings

Ingredients:
- 1 tablespoon olive oil
- 1 clove garlic, peeled and minced
- 1 ½ to 1 ¾ pound rack of lamb
- Salt and pepper to taste
- ¾ cup unsalted macadamia nuts
- 1 tablespoon fresh rosemary, chopped
- 1 tablespoon breadcrumbs
- 1 egg, beaten

Directions:
1. Mix together the olive oil and garlic and brush it all over the rack of lamb. Season with salt and pepper.
2. Preheat the air fryer 250 degrees F for 8 minutes.
3. Chop the macadamia nuts as fine as possible and put them in a bowl.
4. Mix in the rosemary and breadcrumbs and set it aside.
5. Beat the egg in another bowl.
6. Dip the rack in the egg mixture to coat completely.
7. Place the rack in the breadcrumb mixture and coat well.
8. Spray the basket of the air fryer using cooking spray and place the rack inside.
9. Cook at 250 degrees for 25 minutes and then increase to 400 and cook another 5 to 10 minutes or until done.
10. Cover with foil paper for 10 minutes, uncover and separate into chops and serve.

Nutrition:
Calories: 321 |Fat: 9g| Protein: 12g| Fiber: 8.3g

65. Bacon-Wrapped Pork Tenderloin

P Prep Time 5 m | P Cooking Time 15 m | 4 Servings

Ingredients
Pork:
- 1-2 tbsp. Dijon mustard

- 3-4 strips of bacon
- 1 pork tenderloin

Apple Gravy:
- ½ - 1 tsp. Dijon mustard
- 1 tbsp. almond flour
- tbsp. ghee
- 1 chopped onion
- 2-3 Granny Smith apples
- 1 C. vegetable broth

Directions
1. Spread Dijon mustard all over the tenderloin and wrap the meat with strips of bacon.
2. Place into the Air fryer oven, set the temperature to 360°F, and set time to 15 minutes, and cook 10-15 minutes at 360 degrees.
3. To make sauce, heat ghee in a pan and add shallots. Cook 1-2 minutes.
4. Then add apples, cooking 3-5 minutes until softened.
5. Add flour and ghee to make a roux. Add broth and mustard, stirring well to combine.
6. When the sauce starts to bubble, add 1 cup of sautéed apples, cooking till sauce thickens.
7. Once the pork tenderloin is cooked, let it sit 5-10 minutes to rest before slicing.
8. Serve topped with apple gravy.

Nutrition
Calories 552 |Fat 25 g |Protein 29 g |Sugar 6 g

66. Dijon Garlic Pork Tenderloin

P Prep Time 5 m | P Cooking Time 10 m | 6 Servings
Ingredients
- 1 C. breadcrumbs
- Pinch of cayenne pepper
- Crushed garlic cloves
- 2 tbsp. ground ginger
- 2 tbsp. Dijon mustard
- 2 tbsp. raw honey
- tbsp. water
- 2 tsp. salt
- 1 pound pork tenderloin, sliced into 1-inch rounds

Directions
1. With pepper and salt, season all sides of the tenderloin.
2. Combine cayenne pepper, garlic, ginger, mustard, honey, and water until smooth.
3. Dip pork rounds into the honey mixture and then into breadcrumbs, ensuring they all get coated well.
4. Place coated pork rounds into your Air fryer oven.
5. Set temperature to 400°F, and set time to 10 minutes. Cook 10 minutes at 400 degrees. Flip and then cook an additional 5 minutes until golden in color.

Nutrition
Calories 423 |Fat 18 g |Protein 31 g |Sugar 3 g

67. Pork Neck with Salad

P Prep Time 10 m | P Cooking Time 12 m | 2 Servings
Ingredients

For Pork:
- 1 tablespoon soy sauce
- 1 tablespoon fish sauce
- ½ tablespoon oyster sauce
- ½ pound pork neck

For Salad:
- 1 ripe tomato, sliced tickly
- 8-10 Thai shallots, sliced
- 1 scallion, chopped
- 1 bunch fresh basil leaves
- 1 bunch fresh cilantro leaves

For Dressing:
- Tablespoons fish sauce
- 2 tablespoons olive oil
- 1 teaspoon apple cider vinegar
- 1 tablespoon palm sugar
- 2 bird's eye chili
- 1 tablespoon garlic, minced

Directions
For the pork:
1. In a bowl, mix all the ingredients except the pork.
2. Add the pork neck and marinade layer evenly. Refrigerate for about 2-3 hours.
3. Preheat the deep fryer oven to 340 degrees F.
4. Air fry. Place the pork neck in a grill pan. Cook for about 12 minutes.
5. Meanwhile, in a large bowl, combine all of the salad ingredients.
6. In a bowl, add all the dressing ingredients and beat until well combined.
7. Remove the pork neck from the fryer and cut it into the desired slices.
8. Place the pork slices on top of the salad.

Nutrition
Calories 296 |Fat: 20 g |Protein 24 g |Sugar 8 g

68. Chinese Braised Pork Belly

P Prep Time 5 m | P Cooking Time 20 m | 8 Servings

Ingredients
- 1 lb. pork belly, sliced
- 1 tbsp. oyster sauce
- 1 tbsp. sugar
- Red fermented bean curds
- 1 tbsp. red fermented bean curd paste
- 1 tbsp. cooking wine
- 1/2 tbsp. soy sauce
- 1 tsp sesame oil
- 1 cup all-purpose flour

Directions
1. Preheat the Air fryer oven to 390 degrees.
2. In a small bowl, mix up the ingredients together and rub the pork thoroughly with this mixture

3.   Set aside to marinate for at least 30 minutes or preferably overnight for the flavors to permeate the meat
4.   Coat each marinated pork belly slice in flour and place in the Air fryer oven tray
5.   Cook for 20 minutes until crispy and tender.
Nutrition
Calories 409 |Fat 14 g |Protein 19 g |Sugar 9 g

69. Air Fryer Sweet and Sour Pork

P Prep Time 10 m | P Cooking Time 12 m | 6 Servings
Ingredients
- Tbsp. olive oil
- 1/16 tsp. Chinese five-spice
- ¼ tsp. pepper
- ½ tsp. sea salt
- 1 tsp. pure sesame oil
- 2 eggs
- 1 C. almond flour
- 2 pounds pork, sliced into chunks

Sweet and Sour sauce:
- ¼ tsp. sea salt
- ½ tsp. garlic powder
- 1 tbsp. low-sodium soy sauce
- ½ C. rice vinegar
- tbsp. tomato paste
- 1/8 tsp. water
- ½ C. sweetener of choice

Directions
1.   To make the dipping sauce, whisk all sauce ingredients together over medium heat, stirring 5 minutes. Simmer uncovered 5 minutes till thickened.
2.   Meanwhile, combine almond flour, five-spice, pepper, and salt.
3.   In another bowl, mix eggs with sesame oil.
4.   Dredge pork in flour mixture and then in the egg mixture. Shake any excess off before adding to the air fryer rack/basket.
5.   Set temperature to 340°F, and set time to 12 minutes.
6.   Serve with sweet and sour dipping sauce!
Nutrition
Calories 371 |Fat 17 g |Protein 27 g |Sugar 1 g

70. Juicy Pork Ribs Ole

P Prep Time 10 m | P Cooking Time 25 m | 4 Servings
Ingredients
- 1 rack of pork ribs
- 1/2 cup low-fat milk
- 1 tablespoon envelope taco seasoning mix
- 1 can tomato sauce
- 1/2 teaspoon ground black pepper
- 1 teaspoon seasoned salt
- 1 tablespoon cornstarch

- 1 teaspoon canola oil

Directions

1. Place all ingredients in a mixing dish; let them marinate for 1 hour.
2. Cook the marinated ribs approximately 25 minutes at 390 degrees F
3. Work with batches. Enjoy.

Nutrition

Calories 218 |Fat 8 g |Protein 11 g |Sugar 1 g

71. Teriyaki Pork Rolls

P Prep Time 10 m | P Cooking Time 8 m | 6 Servings

Ingredients

- 1 tsp. almond flour
- tbsp. low-sodium soy sauce
- tbsp. mirin
- tbsp. brown sugar
- Thumb-sized amount of ginger, chopped
- Pork belly slices
- Enoki mushrooms

Directions

1. Mix brown sugar, mirin, soy sauce, almond flour, and ginger until brown sugar dissolves.
2. Take pork belly slices and wrap around a bundle of mushrooms. Brush each roll with teriyaki sauce. Chill half an hour.
3. Preheat your Air fryer oven to 350 degrees and add marinated pork rolls.
4. Set temperature to 350°F, and set time to 8 minutes.

Nutrition

Calories 412 |Fat 9 g |Protein 19 g |Sugar 4 g

72. Barbecue Flavored Pork Ribs

P Prep Time 5 m | P Cooking Time 15 m | 6 Servings

Ingredients:

- ¼ cup honey, divided
- ¾ cup BBQ sauce
- 2 tablespoons tomato ketchup
- 1 tablespoon Worcestershire sauce
- 1 tablespoon soy sauce
- ½ teaspoon garlic powder
- Freshly ground white pepper, to taste
- 1¾ pound pork ribs

Directions:

1. Preparing the Ingredients. In a large bowl, mix together 3 tablespoons of honey and remaining ingredients except pork ribs.
2. Refrigerate to marinate for about 20 minutes.
3. Preheat the Air fryer oven to 355 degrees F.
4. Place the ribs in an Air fryer rack/basket.
5. Air Frying. Cook for about 13 minutes.
6. Remove the ribs from the Air fryer oven and coat with remaining honey.
7. Serve hot.

Nutrition:

Calories: 376|Fat: 20g |Protein: 32g| Fiber: 12g

73. Rustic Pork Ribs

P Prep Time 5 m | P Cooking Time 15 m | 4 Servings

Ingredients:

- 1 rack of pork ribs
- 3 tablespoons dry red wine
- 1 tablespoon soy sauce
- 1/2 teaspoon dried thyme
- 1/2 teaspoon onion powder
- 1/2 teaspoon garlic powder
- 1/2 teaspoon ground black pepper
- 1 teaspoon smoke salt
- 1 tablespoon cornstarch
- 1/2 teaspoon olive oil

Directions:

1. Preparing the Ingredients. Begin by preheating your Air fryer oven to 390 degrees F. Place all ingredients in a mixing bowl and let them marinate at least 1 hour.
2. Air Frying. Cook the marinated ribs approximately 25 minutes at 390 degrees F.
3. Serve hot.

Nutrition:

Calories: 326 |Fat: 14g |Protein: 23g| Fiber: 13g

74. Italian Parmesan Breaded Pork Chops

P Prep Time 5 m | P Cooking Time 25 m | 6 Servings

Ingredients:

- 5 (3½- to 5-ounce) pork chops (bone-in or boneless)
- 1 teaspoon Italian seasoning
- Seasoning salt
- Pepper
- ¼ cup all-purpose flour
- 2 tablespoons Italian bread crumbs
- 3 tablespoons finely grated Parmesan cheese
- Cooking oil

Directions:

1. Preparing the Ingredients. Season the pork chops with the Italian seasoning and seasoning salt and pepper to taste.
2. Sprinkle the flour on each sides of the pork chops, then coat both sides with the bread crumbs and Parmesan cheese.
3. Air Frying. Place the pork chops in the Air fryer oven. Stacking them is okay. Spray the pork chops with cooking oil. Set temperature to 360°F. Cook for 6 minutes.
4. Open the Air fryer oven and flip the pork chops. Cook for an additional 6 minutes.
5. Cool before serving. Instead of seasoning salt, you can use either chicken or pork rub for additional flavor. You can find these rubs in the spice aisle of the grocery store.

Nutrition:

Calories: 334| Fat: 7g |Protein: 34g |Fiber: 0g

75. Crispy Breaded Pork Chops

P Prep Time 10 m | P Cooking Time 15 m | 8 Servings

Ingredients:

- 1/8 tsp. pepper
- ¼ tsp. chili powder
- ½ tsp. onion powder
- ½ tsp. garlic powder
- 1 ¼ tsp. sweet paprika
- Tbsp. grated parmesan cheese
- 1/3 C. crushed cornflake crumbs
- ½ C. panko breadcrumbs
- 1 beaten egg
- 6 center-cut boneless pork chops

Directions:

1. Preparing the Ingredients. Ensure that your air fryer is preheated to 400 degrees. Spray the basket with olive oil.
2. With ½ teaspoon salt and pepper, season both sides of pork chops.
3. Combine ¾ teaspoon salt with pepper, chili powder, onion powder, garlic powder, paprika, cornflake crumbs, panko breadcrumbs, and parmesan cheese.
4. Beat egg in another bowl.
5. Dip the pork chops into the egg and then crumb mixture.
6. Add pork chops to air fryer and spritz with olive oil.
7. Air Frying. Set temperature to 400°F, and set time to 12 minutes. Cook 12 minutes, making sure to flip over halfway through the cooking process.
8. Only add 3 chops in at a time and repeat the process with remaining pork chops.

Nutrition:
Calories: 378| Fat: 13g | Protein: 33g |Sugar: 1

76. Caramelized Pork Shoulder

P Prep Time 10 m | P Cooking Time20 m | 8 Servings

Ingredients:

- 1/3 cup soy sauce
- Tablespoons sugar
- 1 tablespoon honey
- 2 pound pork shoulder, cut into 1½-inch thick slices

Directions:

1. Preparing the Ingredients. In a bowl, mix all the ingredients except pork.
2. Add pork and coat with marinade generously.
3. Cover and refrigerate o marinate for about 2-8 hours.
4. Preheat the Air fryer oven to 335 degrees F.
5. Air Frying. Place the pork in an Air fryer rack/basket.
6. Cook for about 10 minutes.
7. Now, set the Air fryer oven to 390 degrees F. Cook for about 10 minutes.

Nutrition:
Calories: 268| Fat: 10g |Protein: 23g |Sugar: 5

77. Roasted Pork Tenderloin

P Prep Time 5 m | P Cooking Time 1 h | 4 Servings

Ingredients:

- 1 (3-pound) pork tenderloin
- Tablespoons extra-virgin olive oil
- 2 garlic cloves, minced
- 1 teaspoon dried basil
- 1 teaspoon dried oregano
- 1 teaspoon dried thyme
- Salt
- Pepper

Directions:
1. Preparation of ingredients. Dip the pork fillet in olive oil.
2. Grate the garlic, basil, oregano, thyme, and salt and pepper to taste throughout the steak.
3. Air fry. Place the steak in the oven of the deep fryer. Cook for 45 minutes.
4. Use a meat thermometer to check for politeness
5. Open the Air Fryer and flip the pork fillet. Cook for 15 more minutes.
6. Take the cooked pork out of the deep fryer and let it rest for 10 minutes before slicing it.

Nutrition:
Calories: 283| Fat: 10g| Protein: 48

78. Bacon Wrapped Pork Tenderloin

P Prep Time 5 m | P Cooking Time 15 m | 4 Servings
Ingredients:
Pork:
- 1-2 tbsp. Dijon mustard
- 3-4 strips of bacon
- 1 pork tenderloin

Apple Gravy:
- ½ - 1 tsp. Dijon mustard
- 1 tbsp. almond flour
- Tbsp. ghee
- 1 chopped onion
- 2-3 Granny Smith apples
- 1 C. vegetable broth

Directions:
1. Preparing the Ingredients. Spread Dijon mustard all over tenderloin and wrap the meat with strips of bacon.
2. Air Frying. Place into the Air fryer oven, set temperature to 360°F, and set time to 15 minutes and cook 10-15 minutes at 360 degrees.
3. To make sauce, heat ghee in a pan and add shallots. Cook 1-2 minutes.
4. Then add apples, cooking 3-5 minutes until softened.
5. Add flour and ghee to make a roux. Add broth and mustard, stirring well to combine.
6. When the sauce starts to bubble, add 1 cup of sautéed apples, cooking till sauce thickens.
7. Once pork tenderloin I cook, allow to sit 5-10 minutes to rest before slicing.
8. Serve topped with apple gravy.

Nutrition:
Calories: 552| Fat: 25g| Protein: 29g |Sugar: 6g

79. Dijon Garlic Pork Tenderloin

P Prep Time 5 m | P Cooking Time 10 m | 6 Servings

Ingredients:
- 1 C. breadcrumbs
- Pinch of cayenne pepper
- Crushed garlic cloves
- 2 tbsp. ground ginger
- 2 tbsp. Dijon mustard
- 2 tbsp. raw honey
- Tbsp. water
- 2 tsp. salt
- 1 pound pork tenderloin, sliced into 1-inch rounds

Directions:
1. Preparing the Ingredients. With pepper and salt, season all sides of tenderloin.
2. Combine cayenne pepper, garlic, ginger, mustard, honey, and water until smooth.
3. Dip pork rounds into the honey mixture and then into breadcrumbs, ensuring they all get coated well.
4. Place coated pork rounds into your Air fryer oven.
5. Air Frying. Set temperature to 400°F, and set time to 10 minutes. Cook 10 minutes at 400 degrees. Flip and then cook an additional 5 minutes until golden in color. **Nutrition:** Calories: 423 |Fat: 18g |Protein: 31g |Sugar: 3g

80. Pork Neck with Salad

P Prep Time 10 m | P Cooking Time 12 m | 2 Servings

Ingredients:

For Pork:
- 1 tablespoon soy sauce
- 1 tablespoon fish sauce
- ½ tablespoon oyster sauce
- ½ pound pork neck

For Salad:
- 1 ripe tomato, sliced tickly
- 8-10 Thai shallots, sliced
- 1 scallion, chopped
- 1 bunch fresh basil leaves
- 1 bunch fresh cilantro leaves

For Dressing:
- Tablespoons fish sauce
- 2 tablespoons olive oil
- 1 teaspoon apple cider vinegar
- 1 tablespoon palm sugar
- 2 bird eye chili
- 1 tablespoon garlic, minced

Directions:
1. Preparation of ingredients. For the pork in a bowl, mix all the ingredients except the pork.
2. Add the pork neck and marinade layer evenly. Refrigerate for about 2-3 hours.
3. Preheat the deep fryer oven to 340 degrees F.
4. Air fry. Place the pork neck in a grill pan. Cook for about 12 minutes.
5. Meanwhile, in a large bowl, combine all of the salad ingredients.

49

6.	In a bowl, add all the dressing ingredients and beat until well combined.
7.	Remove the pork neck from the fryer and cut it into the desired slices.
8.	Place the pork slices on top of the salad.
Nutrition:
Calories: 296 |Fat: 20g |Protein: 24g |Sugar: 8

81. Chinese Braised Pork Belly

P Prep Time 5 m | P Cooking Time 20 m | 8 Servings
Ingredients:
- 1 lb. Pork Belly, sliced
- 1 Tbsp. Oyster Sauce
- 1 Tbsp. Sugar
- Red Fermented Bean Curds
- 1 Tbsp. Red Fermented Bean Curd Paste
- 1 Tbsp. Cooking Wine
- 1/2 Tbsp. Soy Sauce
- 1 Tsp Sesame Oil
- 1 Cup All Purpose Flour

Directions:
1.	Preparing the Ingredients. Preheat the Air fryer oven to 390 degrees.
2.	In a small bowl, mix up the ingredients together and rub the pork thoroughly with this mixture
3.	Set aside to marinate for at least 30 minutes or preferably overnight for the flavors to permeate the meat
4.	Coat each marinated pork belly slice in flour and place in the Air fryer oven tray
5.	Air Frying. Cook for 20 minutes until crispy and tender.
Nutrition:
Calories: 409 |Fat: 14g |Protein: 19g| Sugar: 9

82. Air Fryer Sweet and Sour Pork

P Prep Time 10 m | P Cooking Time 12 m | 6 Servings
Ingredients:
- Tbsp. olive oil
- 1/16 tsp. Chinese Five Spice
- ¼ tsp. pepper
- ½ tsp. sea salt
- 1 tsp. pure sesame oil
- 2 eggs
- 1 C. almond flour
- 2 pounds pork, sliced into chunks
- Sweet and Sour Sauce:
- ¼ tsp. sea salt
- ½ tsp. garlic powder
- 1 tbsp. low-sodium soy sauce
- ½ C. rice vinegar
- Tbsp. tomato paste
- 1/8 tsp. water
- ½ C. sweetener of choice

Directions:

1.   Preparing the Ingredients. To make the dipping sauce, whisk all sauce ingredients together over medium heat, stirring 5 minutes. Simmer uncovered 5 minutes till thickened.

2.   Meanwhile, combine almond flour, five spice, pepper, and salt.

3.   In another bowl, mix eggs with sesame oil.

4.   Dredge pork in flour mixture and then in egg mixture. Shake any excess off before adding to air fryer rack/basket.

5.   Air Frying. Set temperature to 340°F, and set time to 12 minutes.

6.   Serve with sweet and sour dipping sauce!

Nutrition:

Calories: 371 |Fat: 17g |Protein: 27g| Sugar: 1g

83. Juicy Pork Ribs Ole

P Prep Time 10 m | P Cooking Time 25 m | 4 Servings

Ingredients:

- 1 rack of pork ribs
- 1/2 cup low-fat milk
- 1 tablespoon envelope taco seasoning mix
- 1 can tomato sauce
- 1/2 teaspoon ground black pepper
- 1 teaspoon seasoned salt
- 1 tablespoon cornstarch
- 1 teaspoon canola oil

Directions:

1.   Preparing the Ingredients. Place all ingredients in a mixing dish; let them marinate for 1 hour.

2.   Air Frying. Cook the marinated ribs approximately 25 minutes at 390 degrees F

3.   Work with batches. Enjoy.

Nutrition:

Calories: 218 |Fat: 8g |Protein: 11g| Sugar: 1

POULTRY RECIPES

84. Deviled chicken

P Prep Time 10 m | P Cooking Time 40 m | 8 Servings

Ingredients

- tablespoons butter
- cloves garlic, chopped
- 1 cup Dijon mustard
- 1/2 teaspoon cayenne pepper
- 1 1/2 cups panko breadcrumbs
- 3/4 cup parmesan, freshly grated
- 1/4 cup chives, chopped
- teaspoons paprika
- small bone-in chicken thighs, skin removed

Directions:

1 Toss the chicken thighs with crumbs, cheese, chives, butter, and spices in a bowl and mix well to coat.
2 Transfer the chicken along with its spice mix to a baking pan.
3 Press "power button" of air fry oven and turn the dial to select the "air fry" mode.
4 Press the time button and again turn the dial to set the cooking time to 40 minutes.
5 Now push the temp button and rotate the dial to set the temperature at 350 degrees f.
6 Once preheated, place the baking pan inside and close its lid.
7 Serve warm.

Nutrition:

Calories 380| Fat 20 g| Cholesterol 151 mg|Sodium 686 mg|Carbs 33 g|Fiber 1 g|Protein 21 g

85. Marinated chicken parmesan

P Prep Time 10 m | P Cooking Time 20 m | 4 Servings

Ingredients

- cups breadcrumbs
- 1 teaspoon dried oregano
- 1/2 teaspoon garlic powder
- teaspoons paprika
- 1/2 teaspoon salt
- 1/2 teaspoon black pepper
- egg whites
- 1/2 cup skim milk
- 1/2 cup flour
- oz. Chicken breast halves
- Cooking spray
- 1 jar marinara sauce
- 3/4 cup mozzarella cheese, shredded
- tablespoons parmesan, shredded

Directions:

1 Whisk the flour with all the spices in a bowl and beat the eggs in another.
2 Coat the pounded chicken with flour then dip in the egg whites.
3 Dredge the chicken breast through the crumbs well.

4 Spread marinara sauce in a baking dish and place the crusted chicken on it.
5 Drizzle cheese on top of the chicken.
6 Press "power button" of air fry oven and turn the dial to select the "bake" mode.
7 Press the time button and again turn the dial to set the cooking time to 20 minutes.
8 Now push the temp button and rotate the dial to set the temperature at 400 degrees f.
9 Once preheated, place the baking pan inside and close its lid.
10 Serve warm.
Nutrition:
Calories 361|Fat 16.3 g Cholesterol 114 mg|Sodium 515 mg|Carbs 19.3g|Fiber 0.1g|Protein 33.3 g

86. Rosemary lemon chicken

P Prep Time 10 m | P Cooking Time 45 m | 8 Servings
Ingredients
- 4-lb. (1814.37g) Chicken, cut into pieces
- Salt and black pepper, to taste
- Flour for dredging
- tablespoons olive oil
- 1 large onion, sliced
- Peel of ½ lemon
- large garlic cloves, minced
- 1 1/2 teaspoons rosemary leaves
- 1 tablespoon honey
- 1/4 cup lemon juice
- 1 cup chicken broth

Directions:
1 Dredges the chicken through the flour then place in the baking pan.
2 Whisk broth with the rest of the ingredients in a bowl.
3 Pour this mixture over the dredged chicken in the pan.
4 Press "power button" of air fry oven and turn the dial to select the "bake" mode.
5 Press the time button and again turn the dial to set the cooking time to 45 minutes.
6 Now push the temp button and rotate the dial to set the temperature at 400 degrees f.
7 Once preheated, place the baking pan inside and close its lid.
8 Baste the chicken with its sauce every 15 minutes.
9 Serve warm.
Nutrition:
Calories 405|Fat 22.7 g|Cholesterol 4 mg|Sodium 227 mg|Carbs 26.1 g|Fiber 1.4 g|Protein 45.2 g

87. Garlic chicken potatoes

P Prep Time 10 m | P Cooking Time 30 m | 4 Servings
Ingredients
- lbs. (907.185g) Red potatoes, quartered
- tablespoons olive oil
- 1/2 teaspoon cumin seeds
- Salt and black pepper, to taste
- garlic cloves, chopped
- tablespoons brown sugar
- 1 lemon (1/2 juiced and 1/2 cut into wedges)

- Pinch of red pepper flakes
- skinless, boneless chicken breasts
- tablespoons cilantro, chopped

Directions:

1 Place the chicken, lemon, garlic, and potatoes in a baking pan.

2 Toss the spices, herbs, oil, and sugar in a bowl.

3 Add this mixture to the chicken and veggies then toss well to coat.

4 Press "power button" of air fry oven and turn the dial to select the "bake" mode.

5 Press the time button and again turn the dial to set the cooking time to 30 minutes.

6 Now push the temp button and rotate the dial to set the temperature at 400 degrees f.

7 Once preheated, place the baking pan inside and close its lid.

8 Serve warm.

Nutrition:

Calories 545|Fat 36.4 g|Cholesterol 200 mg|Sodium 272mg|Carbs 40.7g|Fiber 0.2g|Protein 42.5 g

88. Chicken potato bake

P Prep Time 10 m | P Cooking Time 25 m | 4 Servings

Ingredients

- potatoes, diced
- 1 tablespoon garlic, minced
- 1.5 tablespoons olive oil
- 1/8 teaspoon salt
- 1/8 teaspoon pepper
- 1.5 lbs. (680.389g) Boneless skinless chicken
- 3/4 cup mozzarella cheese, shredded
- Parsley chopped

Directions:

1 Toss chicken and potatoes with all the spices and oil in a baking pan.

2 Drizzle the cheese on top of the chicken and potato.

3 Press "power button" of air fry oven and turn the dial to select the "bake" mode.

4 Press the time button and again turn the dial to set the cooking time to 25 minutes.

5 Now push the temp button and rotate the dial to set the temperature at 375 degrees f.

6 Once preheated, place the baking pan inside and close its lid.

7 Serve warm.

Nutrition:

Calories 695|Fat 17.5 g|Cholesterol 283mg|Sodium 355mg|Carbs 26.4g|Fiber 1.8g|Protein 117.4g

89. Spanish chicken bake

P Prep Time 10 m | P Cooking Time 25 m | 4 Servings

Ingredients

- ½ onion, quartered
- ½ red onion, quartered
- ½ lb. (226.8g) Potatoes, quartered
- garlic cloves
- tomatoes, quartered
- 1/8 cup chorizo

- ¼ teaspoon paprika powder
- chicken thighs, boneless
- ¼ teaspoon dried oregano
- ½ green bell pepper, julienned
- Salt
- Black pepper

Directions:
1 Toss chicken, veggies, and all the ingredients in a baking tray.
2 Press "power button" of air fry oven and turn the dial to select the "bake" mode.
3 Press the time button and again turn the dial to set the cooking time to 25 minutes.
4 Now push the temp button and rotate the dial to set the temperature at 425 degrees f.
5 Once preheated, place the baking pan inside and close its lid.
6 Serve warm.

Nutrition:
Calories 301|Fat 8.9 g|Cholesterol 57 mg|Sodium 340 mg|Carbs 24.7 g|Fiber 1.2 g|Protein 15.3 g

90. Chicken pasta bake

P Prep Time 10 m | P Cooking Time 22 m | 4 Servings

Ingredients
- 9oz penne, boiled
- 1 onion, roughly chopped
- chicken breasts, cut into strips
- tablespoon olive oil
- 1 tablespoon paprika
- Salt and black pepper
- Sauce
- 1¾oz butter
- 1¾oz plain flour
- 1 pint 6 fly oz. hot milk
- 1 teaspoon dijon mustard
- 3½oz parmesan cheese, grated
- large tomatoes, deseeded and cubed

Directions:
1 Butter a casserole dish and toss chicken with pasta, onion, oil, paprika, salt, and black pepper in it.
2 Prepare the sauce in a suitable pan. Add butter and melt over moderate heat.
3 Stir in flour and whisk well for 2 minutes, then pour in hot milk.
4 Mix until smooth, then add tomatoes, mustard, and cheese.
5 Toss well and pour this sauce over the chicken mix in the casserole dish.
6 Press "power button" of air fry oven and turn the dial to select the "bake" mode.
7 Press the time button and again turn the dial to set the cooking time to 20 minutes.
8 Now push the temp button and rotate the dial to set the temperature at 375 degrees f.
9 Once preheated, place the casserole dish inside and close its lid.
10 Serve warm.

Nutrition:
Calories 548|Fat 22.9 g|Cholesterol 105 mg|Sodium 350mg|Carbs 17.5g|Fiber 6.3g|Protein 40.1 g

91. Creamy chicken casserole

P Prep Time 10 m | P Cooking Time 45 m | 6 Servings

Ingredients

- Chicken and mushroom casserole:
- 1/2 lbs. (1133.98g) Chicken breasts, cut into strips
- 1 1/2 teaspoon salt
- 1/4 teaspoon black pepper
- 1 cup all-purpose flour
- tablespoon olive oil
- 1-lb. (453.592g) White mushrooms, sliced
- 1 medium onion, diced
- garlic cloves, minced
- Sauce:
- tablespoon unsalted butter
- tablespoon all-purpose flour
- 1 1/2 cups chicken broth
- 1 tablespoon lemon juice
- 1 cup half and half cream

Directions:

1 Butter a casserole dish and toss in chicken with mushrooms and all the casserole ingredients.
2 Prepare the sauce in a suitable pan. Add butter and melt over moderate heat.
3 Stir in flour and whisk well for 2 minutes, then pour in milk, lemon juice, and cream.
4 Mix well and pour milk this sauce over the chicken mix in the casserole dish.
5 Press "power button" of air fry oven and turn the dial to select the "bake" mode.
6 Press the time button and again turn the dial to set the cooking time to 45 minutes.
7 Now push the temp button and rotate the dial to set the temperature at 350 degrees f.
8 Once preheated, place the casserole dish inside and close its lid.
9 Serve warm.

Nutrition:

Calories 409|Fat 50.5 g|Cholesterol 58 mg|Sodium 463 mg|Carbs 9.9 g|Fiber 1.5 g|Protein 29.3 g

92. Italian chicken bake

P Prep Time 10 m | P Cooking Time 25 m | 6 Servings

Ingredients:

- ¾ lbs. (340.194g) Chicken breasts
- tablespoons pesto sauce
- ½ (14 oz.) can tomatoes, diced
- 1 cup mozzarella cheese, shredded
- tablespoon fresh basil, chopped

Directions:

1 Place the flattened chicken breasts in a baking pan and top them with pesto.
2 Add tomatoes, cheese, and basil on top of each chicken piece.
3 Press "power button" of air fry oven and turn the dial to select the "bake" mode.
4 Press the time button and again turn the dial to set the cooking time to 25 minutes.
5 Now push the button and rotate the dial to set the temperature at 355 degrees f.
6 Once preheated, place the baking dish inside and close its lid.
7 Serve warm.

Nutrition:
Calories 537|Fat 19.8 g|Cholesterol 10 mg|Sodium 719 mg|Carbs 25.1 g|Fiber 0.9g|Protein 37.8 g

93. Pesto chicken bake

P Prep Time 10 m | P Cooking Time 35 m | 3 Servings
Ingredients
- chicken breasts
- 1 (6 oz.) Jar basil pesto
- medium fresh tomatoes, sliced
- mozzarella cheese slices

Directions:
1 Spread the tomato slices in a casserole dish and top them with chicken.
2 Add pesto and cheese on top of the chicken and spread evenly.
3 Press "power button" of air fry oven and turn the dial to select the "air fry" mode.
4 Press the time button and again turn the dial to set the cooking time to 30 minutes.
5 Now push the temp button and rotate the dial to set the temperature at 350 degrees f.
6 Once preheated, place the casserole dish inside and close its lid.
7 After it is baked, switch the oven to broil mode and broil for 5 minutes.
8 Serve warm.
Nutrition:
Calories 452|Fat 4 g|Cholesterol 65 mg|Sodium 220 mg|Carbs 23.1 g|Fiber 0.3 g|Protein 26g

94. Baked duck

P Prep Time 10 m | P Cooking Time 20 m | 6 Servings
Ingredients
- 1 ½ sprig of fresh rosemary
- ½ nutmeg
- Black pepper
- Juice from 1 orange
- 1 whole duck
- cloves garlic, chopped
- 1 ½ red onions, chopped
- A few stalks celery
- 1 ½ carrot
- cm piece fresh ginger
- 1 ½ bay leaves
- lbs. (907.185g) Piper potatoes
- cups chicken stock

Directions:
1 Place duck in a large cooking pot and add broth along with all the ingredients.
2 Cook this duck for 2 hours on a simmer then transfer to the baking tray.
3 Press "power button" of air fry oven and turn the dial to select the "air fry" mode.
4 Press the time button and again turn the dial to set the cooking time to 20 minutes.
5 Now push the temp button and rotate the dial to set the temperature at 350 degrees f.
6 Once preheated, place the baking tray inside and close its lid.
7 Serve warm.
Nutrition:

Calories 308|Fat 20.5 g|Cholesterol 42 mg|Sodium 688 mg|Carbs 40.3 g|Fiber 4.3 g|Protein 49 g

95. Roasted goose

P Prep Time 10 m | P Cooking Time 40 m | 12 Servings

Ingredients
- lbs. (3628.74g) Goose
- Juice of a lemon
- Salt and pepper
- 1/2 yellow onion, peeled and chopped
- 1 head garlic, peeled and chopped
- 1/2 cup wine
- 1 teaspoon dried thyme

Directions:
1 Place the goose in a baking tray and whisk the rest of the ingredients in a bowl.
2 Pour this thick sauce over the goose and brush it liberally.
3 Press "power button" of air fry oven and turn the dial to select the "air roast" mode.
4 Press the time button and again turn the dial to set the cooking time to 40 minutes.
5 Now push the temp button and rotate to set the temperature at 355 degrees f.
6 Once preheated, place the casserole dish inside and close its lid.
7 Serve warm.

Nutrition:
Calories 231|Fat 20.1 g|Cholesterol 110 mg|Sodium 941mg|Carbs 20.1g|Fiber 0.9g|Protein 14.6 g

96. Christmas roast goose

P Prep Time 10 m | P Cooking Time 60 m | 12 Servings

Ingredients
- goose
- lemons, sliced
- 1 ½ lime, sliced
- ½ teaspoon Chinese five-spice powder
- ½ handful parsley, chopped
- ½ handful sprigs, chopped
- ½ handful thyme, chopped
- ½ handful sage, chopped
- 1 ½ tablespoon clear honey
- ½ tablespoon thyme leaves

Directions:
1 Place the goose in a baking dish and brush it with honey.
2 Set the lemon and lime slices on top of the goose.
3 Add all the herbs and spice powder over the lemon slices.
4 Press "power button" of air fry oven and turn the dial to select the "air roast" mode.
5 Press the time button and again turn the dial to set the cooking time to 60 minutes.
6 Now push the temp button and rotate the dial to set the temperature at 375 degrees f.
7 Once preheated, place the baking dish inside and close its lid.
8 Serve warm.

Nutrition:

Calories 472|Fat 11.1 g|Cholesterol 610mg|Sodium 749mg|Carbs 19.9g|Fiber 0.2g|Protein 13.5 g

97. Honey and Wine Chicken Breasts

P Prep Time 5 m | P Cooking Time 15 m | 4 Servings

Ingredients

- 2 chicken breasts, rinsed and halved
- 1 tablespoon melted butter
- A pinch of salt and 1/2 tsp freshly ground pepper to taste
- 3/4 teaspoon sea salt, or to taste
- 1 teaspoon paprika
- 1 teaspoon dried rosemary
- 2 tablespoons dry white wine
- 1 tablespoon honey

Directions

1. Firstly, pat the chicken breasts dry. Lightly coat them with the melted butter.
2. Then, add the remaining ingredients.
3. Transfer them to the air fryer rack/basket; bake about 15 minutes at 330 degrees F.
Serve warm and enjoy

Nutrition

Calories 189 |Fat: 14g|Protein:11g|Sugar:1 g

98. Crispy Honey Garlic Chicken Wings

P Prep Time 10 m | P Cooking Time 25 m | 8 Servings

Ingredients

- 1/8 C. water
- ½ tsp. salt
- 4 tbsp. minced garlic
- ¼ C. vegan butter
- ¼ C. raw honey
- ¾ C. almond flour
- 16 chicken wings

Directions

1. Rinse off and dry chicken wings well.
2. Spray air fryer rack/basket with olive oil.
3. Coat chicken wings with almond flour and add coated wings to the Air fryer oven.
4. Set temperature to 380°F, and set time to 25 minutes. Cook shaking every 5 minutes.
5. When the timer goes off, cook 5-10 minutes at 400 degrees till the skin becomes crispy and dry.
6. As chicken cooks, melt butter in a saucepan and add garlic. Sauté garlic 5 minutes. Add salt and honey, simmer 20 minutes. Make sure to stir every so often, so the sauce does not burn. Add a bit of water after 15 minutes to ensure the sauce does not harden.
7. Take out chicken wings from the air fryer and coat in sauce. Enjoy!

Nutrition

Calories: 435 |Fat: 19g |Protein:31g |Sugar 6 g

99. Lemon-Pepper Chicken Wings

P Prep Time 10 m | P Cooking Time 20 m | 4 Servings

Ingredients

- 8 whole chicken wings
- Juice of ½ lemon
- ½ teaspoon garlic powder
- 1 teaspoon onion powder
- Salt
- Pepper
- ¼ cup low-fat buttermilk
- ½ cup all-purpose flour
- Cooking oil

Directions

1. Place the wings in a sealed plastic bag. Drizzle the wings with the lemon juice. Season the wings with the garlic powder, onion powder, and salt and pepper to taste.
2. Seal the bag. Shake thoroughly to combine the seasonings and coat the wings.
3. Pour the buttermilk and the flour into separate bowls large enough to dip the wings.
4. Spray the oven rack/basket with cooking oil.
5. One at a time, dip the wings in the buttermilk and then the flour.
6. Place the wings in the oven rack/basket. It is okay to stack them on top of each other. Spray the wings with cooking oil, being sure to spray the bottom layer. Place the tray rack on the middle shelf of the Air fryer oven. Set temperature to 360°F and cook for 5 minutes.
7. Remove the basket and shake it to ensure all of the pieces will cook fully.
8. Return the basket to the Air fryer oven and continue to cook the chicken. Repeat shaking every 5 minutes until a total of 20 minutes has passed.
9. Cool before serving.

Nutrition

Calories: 347 |Fat: 12g |Protein:46g |Fiber:1g

100. Cheesy Chicken in Leek-Tomato Sauce

P Prep Time 10 m | P Cooking Time 20 m | 4 Servings

Ingredients

- Large-sized chicken breasts, cut in half lengthwise
- Salt and ground black pepper, to taste
- Ounces cheddar cheese, cut into sticks
- 1 tablespoon sesame oil
- 1 cup leeks, chopped
- 2 cloves garlic, minced
- 2/3 cup roasted vegetable stock
- 2/3 cup tomato puree
- 1 teaspoon dried rosemary
- 1 teaspoon dried thyme

Directions

1. Firstly, season chicken breasts with the salt and black pepper; place a piece of cheddar cheese in the middle. Then, tie it using a kitchen string; drizzle with sesame oil and reserve.
2. Add the leeks and garlic to the oven-safe bowl.
3. Cook in the Air fryer oven at 390 degrees F for 5 minutes or until tender.
4. Add the reserved chicken. Throw in the other ingredients and cook for 12 to 13 minutes more or until the chicken is done. Enjoy!

101. Mexican Chicken Burgers

P Prep Time 10 m | P Cooking Time 10 m | 6 Servings

Ingredients

- 1 jalapeno pepper
- 1 tsp. cayenne pepper
- 1 tbsp. mustard powder
- 1 tbsp. oregano
- 1 tbsp. thyme
- 3 tbsp. smoked paprika
- 1 beaten egg
- 1 small head of cauliflower
- Chicken breasts

Directions

1. Ensure your Air fryer oven is preheated to 350 degrees.
2. Add seasonings to a blender. Slice cauliflower into florets and add to blender.
3. Pulse till mixture resembles that of breadcrumbs.
4. Take out ¾ of the cauliflower mixture and add to a bowl. Set to the side. In another bowl, beat your egg and set it to the side.
5. Remove skin and bones from chicken breasts and add to blender with remaining cauliflower mixture. Season with pepper and salt.
6. Take out the mixture and form into burger shapes. Roll each patty in cauliflower crumbs, then the egg, and back into crumbs again.
7. Place coated patties into the Air fryer oven. Set temperature to 350°F, and set time to 10 minutes.
8. Flip over at a 10-minute mark. They are done when crispy!

Nutrition

Calories: 234 |Fat: 18g |Protein: 24g |Sugar: 1g

102. Fried Chicken Livers

P Prep Time 5 m | P Cooking Time 10 m | 4 Servings

Ingredients

- 1 pound chicken livers
- 1 cup flour
- 1/2 cup cornmeal
- 2 teaspoons your favorite seasoning blend
- eggs
- 2 tablespoons milk

Directions

1. Clean and rinse the livers, pat dry.
2. Beat eggs in a shallow bowl and mix in milk.
3. In another bowl combine flour, cornmeal, and seasoning, mixing until even.
4. Dip the livers in the egg mix, then toss them in the flour mix.
5. Air-fry at 375 degrees for 10 minutes using your Air fryer oven. Toss at least once halfway through.

Nutrition

Calories 409 |Fat 11g |Protein 36g|Fiber 2g

103. Minty Chicken-Fried Pork Chops

P Prep Time 10 m | P Cooking Time 30 m | 6 Servings

Ingredients

- Medium-sized pork chops, approximately 3.5 ounces each
- 1 cup of breadcrumbs (Panko brand works well)
- 2 medium-sized eggs
- Pinch of salt and pepper
- ½ tablespoon of mint, either dried and ground; or fresh, rinsed and finely chopped

Directions

1.	Cover the basket of the Air fryer oven with a lining of tin foil, leaving the edges uncovered to allow air to circulate through the basket. Preheat the Air fryer oven to 350 degrees.
2.	In a bowl, beat the eggs until fluffy and until the yolks and whites are completely combined and set aside.
3.	In a separate bowl, combine the crumbs, mint, salt, and pepper and set aside. One at a time, dip each raw pork chop into the dry ingredient bowl, coat all sides, then dip it into the wet ingredient bowl, then dip it back into the dry ingredients. This double layer will ensure cooler air. Place the breaded pork chops on the oven rack, in a single flat layer. Place the air fryer rack on the middle shelf of the fryer.
4.	Set the Air Fryer timer to 15 minutes. After 15 minutes the Air Fryer oven will turn off and the pork should cook in the middle and the bread layer should start to brown. Using tweezers, flip each piece of meat over to secure a full pair of pants. Return the fryer to 320 degrees for 15 minutes.
5.	After 15 minutes, when the fryer is off, remove the fried pork chops with tongs and place them in a source. Eat as fresh as you can, and enjoy it!

Nutrition

Calories 213 |Fat 9g |Protein 12g |Fiber 3g

104. Crispy Southern Fried Chicken

P Prep Time 10 m | P Cooking Time 25 m | 4 Servings

Ingredients

- 1 tsp. cayenne pepper
- 2 tbsp. mustard powder
- 2 tbsp. oregano
- 2 tbsp. thyme
- 3 tbsp. coconut milk
- 1 beaten egg
- ¼ C. cauliflower
- ¼ C. gluten-free oats
- 8 chicken drumsticks

Directions

1.	Ensure the Air fryer oven is preheated to 350 degrees.
2.	Lay out the chicken and season with pepper and salt on all sides.
3.	Add all other ingredients to a blender, blending till a smooth-like breadcrumb mixture is created. Place in a bowl and add a beaten egg to another bowl.
4.	Dip chicken into breadcrumbs, then into the egg, and breadcrumbs once more.
5.	Place coated drumsticks into the Air fryer oven. Set temperature to 350°F, and set time to 20 minutes, and cook 20 minutes. Bump up the temperature to 390 degrees and cook another 5 minutes till crispy.

Nutrition

Calories 504 |Fat 18g|Protein 35g|Sugar 5g

105. Tex-Mex Turkey Burgers

P Prep Time 10 m | P Cooking Time 15 m | 4 Servings

Ingredients
- ⅓ cup finely crushed corn tortilla chips
- 1 egg, beaten
- ¼ cup salsa
- ⅓ cup shredded pepper Jack cheese
- Pinch salt
- Freshly ground black pepper
- 1 pound ground turkey
- 1 tablespoon olive oil
- 1 teaspoon paprika

Directions
1. In a small bowl, combine the tortilla chips, egg, salsa, cheese, salt, and pepper, and mix well.
2. Add the turkey and mix gently but thoroughly with clean hands.
3. Form the meat mixture into patties about ½ inch thick. Make an indentation in the center of each patty with your thumb, so the burgers don't puff up while cooking.
4. Brush the patties on each side with the olive oil and sprinkle with paprika.
5. Put in the oven rack/basket. Place the tray rack on the middle shelf of the Air fryer oven. Grill for 14 to 16 minutes or until the meat registers at least 165°F.

Nutrition
Calories 354|Fat 21g|Protein 36g|Fiber 2g

106. Air Fryer Turkey Breast

P Prep Time 5 m | P Cooking Time 60 m | 6 Servings

Ingredients
- Pepper and salt
- 1 oven-ready turkey breast
- Turkey seasonings of choice

Directions
1. Preheat the Air fryer oven to 350 degrees.
2. Season turkey with pepper, salt, and other desired seasonings.
3. Place turkey in the oven rack/basket. Place the tray Rack on the middle-shelf of the Air fryer oven.
4. Set temperature to 350°F, and set time to 60 minutes. Cook 60 minutes. The meat should be at 165 degrees when done.
5. Allow resting 10-15 minutes before slicing. Enjoy!

Nutrition
Calories 212 |Fat 12g|Protein 24g|Sugar 0g

107. Mustard Chicken Tenders

P Prep Time 5 m | P Cooking Time 20 m | 4 Servings

Ingredients
- ½ C. coconut flour
- 1 tbsp. spicy brown mustard

- Beaten eggs
- 1 pound of chicken tenders

Directions
1. Season tenders with pepper and salt.
2. Place a thin layer of mustard onto tenders and then dredge in flour and dip in egg.
3. Add to the Air fryer oven, set the temperature to 390°F, and set time to 20 minutes.

Nutrition
Calories 403|Fat 20g|Protein 22g|Sugar 4g

108. Chicken Nuggets

P Prep Time 10 m | P Cooking Time 20 m | 4 Servings
Ingredients
- 1 pound boneless, skinless chicken breasts
- Chicken seasoning or rub
- Salt
- Pepper
- Eggs
- Tablespoons bread crumbs
- Tablespoons panko bread crumbs
- Cooking oil

Directions
1. Cut the chicken breasts into 1-inch pieces.
2. In a large bowl, add together the chicken pieces with the chicken seasoning, salt, and pepper.
3. In a small bowl, beat the eggs. In another bowl, combine breadcrumbs and countertop.
4. Dip the chicken pieces in the eggs and then the breadcrumbs.
5. Place the pepitas in the deep fryer. Don't overdo the basket. Cook in batches. Drizzle the seeds with cooking oil.
6. Cook for 4 minutes. Open the air fryer oven and shake the basket. Set temperature to 360°F. Cook for an additional 4 minutes. Remove the cooked nuggets from the air fryer oven, then repeat steps 5 and 6 for the remaining chicken nuggets. Cool before serving.

Nutrition
Calories 206 |Fat 5g|Protein 31g |Fiber 1g

109. Cheesy Chicken Fritters

P Prep Time 5 m | P Cooking Time 20 m | 17 Servings
Ingredients
Chicken Fritters:
- ½ tsp. salt
- 1/8 tsp. pepper
- 1 ½ tbsp. fresh dill
- 1 1/3 C. shredded mozzarella cheese
- 1/3 C. coconut flour
- 1/3 C. vegan mayo
- 2 eggs
- 1 ½ pounds chicken breasts
Garlic Dip:
- 1/8 tsp. pepper

64

- ¼ tsp. salt
- ½ tbsp. lemon juice
- 1 pressed garlic cloves
- 1/3 C. vegan mayo

Directions

1.   Slice chicken breasts into 1/3" pieces and place in a bowl. Add all remaining fritter ingredients to the bowl and stir well. Cover and chill 2 hours or overnight.
2.   Ensure your air fryer is preheated to 350 degrees. Spray basket with a bit of olive oil.
3.   Add marinated chicken to the air fryer oven. Set temperature to 350°F, and set time to 20 minutes and cook 20 minutes, making sure to turn halfway through the cooking process.
4.   To make the dipping sauce, combine all the dip ingredients until smooth.

Nutrition

Calories 467|Fat 27g|Protein 21g |Sugar 3g

110. Air Fryer Chicken Parmesan

P Prep Time 5 m | P Cooking Time 9 m | 4 Servings

Ingredients

- ½ C. keto marinara
- tbsp. mozzarella cheese
- 1 tbsp. melted ghee
- tbsp. grated parmesan cheese
- tbsp. gluten-free seasoned breadcrumbs
- 8-ounce chicken breasts

Directions

1.   Ensure air fryer is preheated to 360 degrees. Spray the basket with olive oil.
2.   Mix parmesan cheese and breadcrumbs together. Melt ghee.
3.   Brush melted ghee onto the chicken and dip into breadcrumb mixture.
4.   Place coated chicken in the air fryer and top with olive oil.
5.   Set temperature to 360°F, and set time to 6 minutes. Cook 2 breasts for 6 minutes and top each breast with a tablespoon of sauce and 1½ tablespoons of mozzarella cheese. Cook another 3 minutes to melt the cheese.
6.   Keep cooked pieces warm as you repeat the process with remaining breasts.

Nutrition

Calories 251|Fat 10g|Protein 31g|Sugar 0g

111. Pretzel Crusted Chicken With Spicy Mustard Sauce

P Prep Time 15 m | P Cooking Time 20 m | 6 Servings

Ingredients:

- 2 eggs
- 1 ½ pound chicken breasts, boneless, skinless, cut into bite-sized chunks
- 1/2 cup crushed pretzels
- 1 teaspoon shallot powder
- 1 teaspoon paprika
- Sea salt and ground black pepper, to taste
- 1/2 cup vegetable broth
- 1 tablespoon cornstarch
- 3 tablespoons Worcestershire sauce
- 3 tablespoons tomato paste

- 1 tablespoon apple cider vinegar
- 2 tablespoons olive oil
- 2 garlic cloves, chopped
- 1 jalapeno pepper, minced
- 1 teaspoon yellow mustard

Directions:
1.   Start by preheating your Air Fryer to 390 degrees F.
2.   In a mixing dish, whisk the eggs until frothy; toss the chicken chunks into the whisked eggs and coat well.
3.   In another dish, combine the crushed pretzels with shallot powder, paprika, salt and pepper. Then, lay the chicken chunks in the pretzel mixture; turn it over until well coated.
4.   Place the chicken pieces in the air fryer basket. Cook the chicken for 12 minutes, shaking the basket halfway through.
5.   Meanwhile, whisk the vegetable broth with cornstarch, Worcestershire sauce, tomato paste, and apple cider vinegar.
6.   Preheat a cast-iron skillet over medium flame. Heat the olive oil and sauté the garlic with jalapeno pepper for 30 to 40 seconds, stirring frequently.
7.   Add the cornstarch mixture and let it simmer until the sauce has thickened a little. Now, add the air-fried chicken and mustard; let it simmer for 2 minutes more or until heated through.
8.   Serve immediately and enjoy!

Nutrition:
357 Calories 17.6g Fat 20.3g Carbs 28.1g Protein 2.8g Sugars

112. Chinese-Style Sticky Turkey Thighs

P Prep Time 20 m | P Cooking Time 35 m | 6 Servings

Ingredients:
- 1 tablespoon sesame oil
- 2 pounds turkey thighs
- 1 teaspoon Chinese Five-spice powder
- 1 teaspoon pink Himalayan salt
- 1/4 teaspoon Sichuan pepper
- 6 tablespoons honey
- 1 tablespoon Chinese rice vinegar
- 2 tablespoons soy sauce
- 1 tablespoon sweet chili sauce
- 1 tablespoon mustard

Directions:
1.   Preheat your Air Fryer to 360 degrees F.
2.   Brush the sesame oil all over the turkey thighs. Season them with spices.
3.   Cook for 23 minutes, turning over once or twice. Make sure to work in batches to ensure even cooking
4.   In the meantime, combine the remaining ingredients in a wok (or similar type pan) that is preheated over medium-high heat. Cook and stir until the sauce reduces by about a third.
5.   Add the fried turkey thighs to the wok; gently stir to coat with the sauce.
6.   Let the turkey rest for 10 minutes before slicing and serving. Enjoy!

Nutrition:
279 Calories 10.1g Fat 19g Carbs 27.7g Protein 17.9g Sugars

113. Easy Hot Chicken Drumsticks

P Prep Time 40 m | P Cooking Time 30 m | 6 Servings

Ingredients:

- 6 chicken drumsticks
- Sauce:
- 6 ounces hot sauce
- 3 tablespoons olive oil
- 3 tablespoons tamari sauce
- 1 teaspoon dried thyme
- 1/2 teaspoon dried oregano

Directions:

1. Spritz the sides and bottom of the cooking basket with a nonstick cooking spray.
2. Cook the chicken drumsticks at 380 degrees F for 35 minutes, flipping them over halfway through.
3. Meanwhile, heat the hot sauce, olive oil, tamari sauce, thyme, and oregano in a pan over medium-low heat; reserve.
4. Drizzle the sauce over the prepared chicken drumsticks; toss to coat well and serve. Bon appétit!

Nutrition:

280 Calories 18.7g Fat 2.6g Carbs 24.1g Protein 1.4g Sugars

114. Crunchy Munchy Chicken Tenders With Peanuts

P Prep Time 25 m | P Cooking Time 20 m | 4 Servings

Ingredients:

- 1 ½ pounds chicken tenderloins
- 2 tablespoons peanut oil
- 1/2 cup tortilla chips, crushed
- Sea salt and ground black pepper, to taste
- 1/2 teaspoon garlic powder
- 1 teaspoon red pepper flakes
- 2 tablespoons peanuts, roasted and roughly chopped

Directions:

1. Start by preheating your Air Fryer to 360 degrees F.
2. Brush the chicken tenderloins with peanut oil on all sides.
3. In a mixing bowl, thoroughly combine the crushed chips, salt, black pepper, garlic powder, and red pepper flakes. Dredge the chicken in the breading, shaking off any residual coating.
4. Lay the chicken tenderloins into the cooking basket. Cook for 12 to 13 minutes or until it is no longer pink in the center. Work in batches; an instant-read thermometer should read at least 165 degrees F.
5. Serve garnished with roasted peanuts. Bon appétit!

Nutrition:

343 Calories 16.4g Fat 10.6g Carbs 36.8g Protein 1g Sugar

FISH AND SEAFOOD RECIPES

115. Prawn Momo's Recipe

P Prep Time 15 m | P Cooking Time 25 m | 4 Servings

Ingredients:
- 1 ½ cup all-purpose flour
- ½ tsp. salt
- 5 tbsp. water
- For filling:
- 2 cups minced prawn
- 2 tbsp. oil
- 2 tsp. ginger-garlic paste
- 2 tsp. soya sauce
- 2 tsp. vinegar

Directions:
1. Squeeze the dough and cover it with plastic wrap and set aside. Next, cook the ingredients for the filling and try to ensure that the prawn is covered well with the sauce. Roll the dough and cut it into a square.
2. Place the filling in the center. Now, wrap the dough to cover the filling and pinch the edges together. Pre heat the smart oven at 200° F for 5 minutes. Place the wontons in the fry basket and close it. Let them cook at the same temperature for another 20 minutes. Recommended sides are chili sauce or ketchup.

Nutrition:
Calories: 300 |Fat: 11g| Protein: 35g| Sugar: 6

116. Fish club Classic Sandwich

P Prep Time 10 m | P Cooking Time 20 m | 3 Servings

Ingredients:
- 2 slices of white bread
- 1 tbsp. softened butter
- 1 tin tuna
- 1 small capsicum
- For Barbeque Sauce:
- ¼ tbsp. Worcestershire sauce
- ½ tsp. olive oil
- ½ flake garlic crushed
- ¼ cup chopped onion
- ¼ tsp. mustard powder
- ½ tbsp. sugar
- ¼ tbsp. red chili sauce
- 1 tbsp. tomato ketchup
- ½ cup water.
- Salt and black pepper to taste

Directions:
1. Remove the edges of the slice bread. Now cut the slices horizontally. Cook the ingredients for the sauce and wait till it thickens. Now, add the fish to the sauce and stir till it obtains the flavors. Roast the capsicum and peel the skin off. Cut the capsicum into slices.

2. Mix the ingredients and apply it to the bread slices. Pre-heat the smart oven for 5 minutes at 300 Fahrenheit.

3. Open the basket of the Fryer and place the prepared Classic Sandwiches in it such that no two Classic Sandwiches are touching each other. Now keep the fryer at 250 degrees for around 15 minutes. Turn the Classic Sandwiches in between the cooking process to cook both slices. Serve the Classic Sandwiches with tomato ketchup or mint sauce.

Nutrition:
Calories: 232 |Fat: 22g| Protein: 25g| Sugar: 5

117. Prawn Fried Baked Pastry

P Prep Time 15 m | P Cooking Time 35 m | 4 Servings

Ingredients:

- 1 ½ cup all-purpose flour
- 2 tbsp. unsalted butter
- 2 green chilies that are finely chopped or mashed
- Add a lot of water to make the dough stiff and firm
- A pinch of salt to taste
- 1 lb. prawn
- ¼ cup boiled peas
- ½ tsp. cumin
- 1 tsp. coarsely crushed coriander
- 1 dry red chili broken into pieces
- A small amount of salt (to taste)
- ½ tsp. dried mango powder
- 1 tsp. powdered ginger
- ½ tsp. red chili power.
- 1-2 tbsp. coriander.

Directions:

1. You will first need to make the outer covering. In a large bowl, add the flour, butter and enough water to knead it into dough that is stiff. Transfer this to a container and leave it to rest for five minutes. Place a pan on medium flame and add the oil. Roast the mustard seeds and once roasted, add the coriander seeds and the chopped dry red chilies. Add all the dry ingredients for the filling and mix the ingredients well.

2. Add a little water and continue to mix the ingredients. Make small balls from the dough and wrap them. Cut the wrapped dough in half and spread a little water on the edges to help you fold the halves into a cone. Add the filling to the cone and close the samosa. Preheat the Smart Oven for about 5 to 6 minutes at 300 Fahrenheit. Place all the samosas in the frying pan and close the basket properly.

3. Keep the Smart Oven at 200 degrees for another 20 to 25 minutes. Around half point, open the basket and turn the samosas for even cooking. After that, fry at 250 degrees for about 10 minutes to give them the desired golden-brown color. Serve hot. Recommended sides are tamarind or mint sauce.

Nutrition:
Calories: 132 |Fat: 1g |Protein: 15g |Sugar: 9

118. Fish Spicy Lemon Kebab

P Prep Time 10 m | P Cooking Time 25 m | 3 Servings

Ingredients:

- 1 lb. boneless fish roughly chopped
- 3 onions chopped
- 5 green chilies-roughly chopped
- 1 ½ tbsp. ginger paste
- 1 ½ tsp garlic paste
- 1 ½ tsp salt
- 3 tsp lemon juice
- 2 tsp garam masala
- 4 tbsp. chopped coriander
- 3 tbsp. cream
- 2 tbsp. coriander powder
- 4 tbsp. fresh mint chopped
- 3 tbsp. chopped capsicum
- 3 eggs
- 2 ½ tbsp. white sesame seeds

Directions:

1.   Take all the ingredients mentioned under the first heading and mix them in a bowl. Grind them thoroughly to make a smooth paste. Take the eggs in a different bowl and beat them. Add a pinch of salt and leave them aside. Take a flat plate and in it mix the sesame seeds and breadcrumbs. Mold the mixture of fish into small balls and flatten them into round and flat kebabs. Dip these kebabs in the egg and salt mixture and then in the mixture of breadcrumbs and sesame seeds. Leave these kebabs in the fridge for an hour or so to set.

2.   Pre heat the smart oven at 160 degrees Fahrenheit for around 5 minutes. Place the kebabs in the basket and let them cook for another 25 minutes at the same temperature. Turn the kebabs over in between the cooking process to get a uniform cook. Serve the kebabs with mint sauce.

Nutrition:

Calories: 432| Fat: 3g |Protein: 22g |Sugar: 1

119. Fish Oregano Fingers

P Prep Time 10 m | P Cooking Time 25 m | 4 Servings

Ingredients:

- ½ lb. firm white fish fillet cut into Oregano Fingers
- 1 tbsp. lemon juice
- 2 cups of dry breadcrumbs
- 1 cup oil for frying
- 1 ½ tbsp. ginger-garlic paste
- 3 tbsp. lemon juice
- 2 tsp salt
- 1 ½ tsp pepper powder
- 1 tsp red chili
- 3 eggs
- 5 tbsp. corn flour
- 2 tsp tomato ketchup

Directions:

1.   Rub a little lemon juice on the Oregano Fingers and set aside. Wash the fish after an hour and pat dry. Make the marinade and transfer the Oregano Fingers into the marinade. Allow them

to dry on a plate for fifteen minutes. Now cover the Oregano Fingers with the crumbs and set aside to dry for fifteen minutes.

2.   Pre heat the smart oven at 160 degrees Fahrenheit for 5 minutes or so. Keep the fish in the fry basket now and close it properly.

3.   Let the Oregano Fingers cook at the same temperature for another 25 minutes. In between the cooking process, toss the fish once in a while to avoid burning the food. Serve either with tomato ketchup or chili sauce. Mint sauce also works well with the fish.

Nutrition:

Calories: 234 |Fat: 3g| Protein: 35g| Sugar: 0

120. Prawn Grandma's Easy to Cook Wontons

P Prep Time 5 m | P Cooking Time 20 m | 3 Servings

Ingredients:

- 1 ½ cup all-purpose flour
- ½ tsp. salt
- 5 tbsp. water
- 2 cups minced prawn
- 2 tbsp. oil
- 2 tsp. ginger-garlic paste
- 2 tsp. soya sauce
- 2 tsp. vinegar

Directions:

1.   Squeeze out the dough and cover it with plastic wrap and set it aside. Then cook the ingredients for the filling and try to make sure the shrimp are well coated with the sauce. Roll out the dough and place the filling in the center.

2.   Now, roll the dough to cover the filling and bring the edges together. Preheat the Smart Oven to 200 ° F for 5 minutes. Place the wontons in the pan and close it. Let them cook at equal temperature for another 20 minutes. Recommended sides are chili sauce or ketchup.

Nutrition:

Calories: 423| Fat: 20g |Protein: 20g |Sugar: 2

121. Tuna Sandwich

P Prep Time 5 m | P Cooking Time 15 m | 4 Servings

Ingredients:

- 2 slices of white bread
- 1 tbsp. softened butter
- 1 tin tuna
- 1 small capsicum
- For Barbeque Sauce:
- ¼ tbsp. Worcestershire sauce
- ½ tsp. olive oil
- ¼ tsp. mustard powder
- ½ flake garlic crushed
- ¼ cup chopped onion
- ½ tbsp. sugar
- 1 tbsp. tomato ketchup
- ½ cup water.
- ¼ tbsp. red chili sauce

- Salt and black pepper to taste

Directions:

1. Remove the edges of the slices bread. Now cut the slices horizontally. Cook the ingredients for the sauce and wait till it thickens. Now, add the lamb to the sauce and stir till it obtains the flavors. Roast the capsicum and peel the skin off. Cut the capsicum into slices. Mix the ingredients and apply it to the bread slices.

2. Pre-heat the smart oven for 5 minutes at 300 Fahrenheit. Open the basket of the Fryer and place the prepared Classic Sandwiches in it such that no two Classic Sandwiches are touching each other. Now keep the fryer at 250 degrees for around 15 minutes. Turn the Classic Sandwiches in between the cooking process to cook both slices. Serve the Classic Sandwiches with tomato ketchup or mint sauce.

Nutrition:

Calories: 460 |Fat: 1g| Protein: 11g |Sugar: 5

122. Salmon Tandoor

P Prep Time 10 m | P Cooking Time 20 m | 5 Servings

Ingredients:

- 2 lb. boneless salmon filets
- 1st Marinade:
- 3 tbsp. vinegar or lemon juice
- 2 or 3 tsp. paprika
- 1 tsp. black pepper
- 1 tsp. salt
- 3 tsp. ginger-garlic paste
- 2nd Marinade:
- 1 cup yogurt
- 4 tsp. tandoori masala
- 2 tbsp. dry fenugreek leaves
- 1 tsp. black salt
- 1 tsp. chat masala
- 1 tsp. garam masala powder
- 1 tsp. red chili powder
- 1 tsp. salt
- 3 drops of red color

Directions:

1. Make the first marinade and soak the fileted salmon in it for four hours. While this is happening, make the second marinade and soak the salmon in it overnight to let the flavors blend. Pre heat the smart oven at 160 degrees Fahrenheit for 5 minutes.

2. Put the oregano fingers in the pan and close it. Let them cook at the equal temperature for another 15 minutes or so. Toss the oregano fingers well so that they are well cooked. Serve with mint sauce.

Nutrition:

Calories: 187 |Fat: 2g |Protein: 30g|Sugar: 0

123. Carp Best Homemade Croquette

P Prep Time 15 m | P Cooking Time 25 m | 3 Servings

Ingredients:

- 1 lb. Carp filets

- 3 onions chopped
- 5 green chilies-roughly chopped
- 1 ½ tbsp. ginger paste
- 1 ½ tsp garlic paste
- 1 ½ tsp salt
- 3 tsp lemon juice
- 2 tsp garam masala
- 4 tbsp. chopped coriander
- 3 tbsp. cream
- 2 tbsp. coriander powder
- 4 tbsp. fresh mint chopped
- 3 tbsp. chopped capsicum
- 3 eggs
- 2 ½ tbsp. white sesame seeds

Directions:
1. Take all the ingredients mentioned under the first heading and mix them in a bowl. Grind them thoroughly to make a smooth paste. Take the eggs in a different bowl and beat them. Add a pinch of salt and leave them aside. Mold the fish mixture into small balls and flatten them into round and flat Best Homemade Croquettes. Dip these Best Homemade Croquettes in the egg and salt mixture and then in the mixture of breadcrumbs and sesame seeds.
2. Leave these Best Homemade Croquettes in the fridge for an hour or so to set. Pre heat the smart oven at 160 degrees Fahrenheit for around 5 minutes. Place the Best Homemade Croquettes in the basket and let them cook for another 25 minutes at the same temperature. Turn the Best Homemade Croquettes over in between the cooking process to get a uniform cook. Serve the Best Homemade Croquettes with mint sauce.

Nutrition:
Calories: 209 |Fat: 4g |Protein: 49g |Sugar: 1

124. Shrimp Momo's Recipe

P Prep Time 10 m | P Cooking Time 20 m | 7 Servings

Ingredients:
- 1 ½ cup all-purpose flour
- ½ tsp. salt
- 5 tbsp. water
- For filling:
- 2 cups minced shrimp
- 2 tbsp. oil
- 2 tsp. ginger-garlic paste
- 2 tsp. soya sauce
- 2 tsp. vinegar

Directions:
1. Squeeze out the dough and cover it with plastic wrap and set it aside. Then cook the ingredients for the filling and try to make sure the shrimp are well coated with the sauce. Roll up the dough and cut it into squares. Place the filling in the center.
2. Now, roll the dough to cover the filling and bring the edges together. Preheat the Smart Oven to 200 ° F for 5 minutes. Place the wontons in the pan and close it. Let them cook at the equal temperature for another 20 minutes. Recommended sides are chili sauce or ketchup.

Nutrition:

Calories: 103 |Fat: 0g| Protein: 34g| Sugar: 11

125. Salmon fries

P Prep Time 5 m | P Cooking Time 15 m | 3 Servings
Ingredients:
- 1 lb. boneless salmon filets
- 2 cup dry breadcrumbs
- 2 tsp. oregano
- 2 tsp. red chili flakes
- 1 ½ tbsp. ginger-garlic paste
- 4 tbsp. lemon juice
- 2 tsp. salt
- 1 tsp. pepper powder
- 1 tsp. red chili powder
- tbsp. corn flour
- 4 eggs

Directions:
1 Mix each and every ingredients for the marinade and put the salmon fillets and leave to rest overnight. Mix the toast, oregano, and red chili flakes well and place the marinated oregano fingers in this mixture. Cover with cling film and leave until served.
2 Preheat the smart oven to 160 degrees Fahrenheit for 5 minutes.
3 Put the oregano fingers in the pan and close it. Let them cook at the equal temperature for another 15 minutes or so. Toss the oregano fingers well so that they are well cooked.
Nutrition:
Calories: 300 |Fat: 3g |Protein: 16g |Sugar: 2

126. Oyster Club Sandwich

P Prep Time 10 m | P Cooking Time 15 m | 4 Servings
Ingredients:
- 2 slices of white bread
- 1 tbsp. softened butter
- ½ lb. shelled oyster
- 1 small capsicum
- For Barbeque Sauce:
- ¼ tbsp. Worcestershire sauce
- ½ tsp. olive oil
- ½ flake garlic crushed
- ¼ cup chopped onion
- ¼ tsp. mustard powder
- 1 tbsp. tomato ketchup
- ½ tbsp. sugar
- ¼ tbsp. red chili sauce
- ½ cup water.
- Salt and black pepper to taste

Directions:
1 Remove the edges of the slice bread. Now cut the slices horizontally. Cook the ingredients for the sauce and wait till it thickens. Now, add the oyster to the sauce and stir till it obtains the flavors.

74

2 Roast the capsicum and peel the skin off. Cut the capsicum into slices. Mix all ingredients together and apply it to the bread slices. Pre-heat the smart oven for 5 minutes at 300 Fahrenheit. Open the basket of the Fryer and place the prepared Classic Sandwiches in it such that no two Classic Sandwiches are touching each other. Now keep the fryer at 250 degrees for around 15 minutes.

3 Turn the Classic Sandwiches in between the cooking process to cook both slices. Serve the Classic Sandwiches with tomato ketchup or mint sauce.

Nutrition:
Calories: 407 |Fat: 10g |Protein: 31g |Sugar: 11

127. Cheese Carp Fries

P Prep Time 15 m | P Cooking Time 25 m | 4 Servings

Ingredients:
- 1 lb. carp Oregano Fingers
- Ingredients for the marinade:
- 1 tbsp. olive oil
- 1 tsp. mixed herbs
- ½ tsp. red chili flakes
- A pinch of salt to taste
- 1 tbsp. lemon juice
- For the garnish:
- 1 cup melted cheddar cheese

Directions:
1 Take all the ingredients mentioned in the heading "For the marinade" and mix well. Cook the oregano fingers and dip them in the marinade.

2 Preheat the smart oven for about 5 minutes at 300 Fahrenheit. Take the basket out of the fryer and place the tent in it. Close the basket. Now keep the fryer at 220 Fahrenheit for 20 to 25 minutes.

3 Between the processes, toss the potatoes two or three times so they are cooked through. Towards the rare end of the cooking process (the last 2 minutes or so), sprinkle the melted cheddar cheese over the potatoes and serve hot.

Nutrition:
Calories: 502 |Fat: 22g |Protein: 40g |Sugar: 14g

128. Seafood Pizza

P Prep Time 10 m | P Cooking Time 22 m | 4 Servings

Ingredients:
- One pizza base
- Grated pizza cheese (mozzarella cheese preferably) for topping
- Some pizza topping sauce
- Use cooking oil for brushing and topping purposes
- Ingredients for topping:
- 2 onions chopped
- 2 cups mixed seafood
- 2 capsicums chopped
- 2 tomatoes that have been deseeded and chopped
- 1 tbsp. (optional) mushrooms/corns
- 2 tsp. pizza seasoning

- Some cottage cheese that has been cut into small cubes (optional)

Directions:

1 Put the pizza base in a pre-heated smart oven for around 5 minutes. (Pre heated to 340 Fahrenheit). Take out the base. Pour some pizza sauce on top of the base at the center. Using a spoon spread the sauce over the base making sure that you leave some gap around the circumference. Grate some mozzarella cheese and sprinkle it over the sauce layer. Take all the vegetables and the seafood and mix them in a bowl. Add some oil and seasoning.

2 Also add some salt and pepper according to taste. Mix them properly. Put this topping over the layer of cheese on the pizza. Now sprinkle some more grated cheese and pizza seasoning on top of this layer. Pre heat the smart oven at 250 Fahrenheit for around 5 minutes.

3 Open the fry basket and place the pizza inside. Close the basket and keep the fryer at 170 degrees for another 10 minutes. If you feel that it is undercooked you may put it at the same temperature for another 2 minutes or so.

Nutrition:

Calories: 116 |Fat: 23g| Protein: 29g| Sugar: 1

129. Prawn Momo's Recipe

P Prep Time 15 m | P Cooking Time 25 m | 4 Servings

Ingredients

- 1 ½ cup all-purpose flour
- ½ tsp. salt
- 5 tbsp. water

For filling:

- 2 cups minced prawn
- 2 tbsp. oil
- 2 tsp. ginger-garlic paste
- 2 tsp. soya sauce
- 2 tsp. vinegar

Directions

1. Squeeze the dough and cover it with plastic wrap and set aside. Next, cook the ingredients for the filling and try to ensure that the prawn is covered well with the sauce. Roll the dough and cut it into a square.

2. Place the filling in the center. Now, wrap the dough to cover the filling and pinch the edges together. Preheat the Breville smart oven at 200° F for 5 minutes. Place the wontons in the fry basket and close it. Let them cook at the same temperature for another 20 minutes. Recommended sides are chili sauce or ketchup.

Nutrition

Calories 300 |Fat 11 g |Protein 35 g |Sugar 6 g

130. Fish Club Classic Sandwich

P Prep Time 10 m | P Cooking Time 20 m | 3 Servings

Ingredients

- 2 slices of white bread
- 1 tbsp. softened butter
- 1 tin tuna
- 1 small capsicum

For Barbeque Sauce:

- ¼ tbsp. Worcestershire sauce

76

- ½ tsp. olive oil
- ½ flake garlic crushed
- ¼ cup chopped onion
- ¼ tsp. mustard powder
- ½ tbsp. sugar
- ¼ tbsp. red chili sauce
- 1 tbsp. tomato ketchup
- ½ cup water.
- Salt and black pepper to taste

Directions

1. Remove the edges of the sliced bread. Now cut the slices horizontally. Cook the ingredients for the sauce and wait till it thickens. Now, add the fish to the sauce and stir till it obtains the flavors. Roast the capsicum and peel the skin off. Cut the capsicum into slices.

2. Mix the ingredients and apply it to the bread slices. Pre-heat the Breville smart oven for 5 minutes at 300 Fahrenheit.

3. Open the basket of the Fryer and place the prepared classic sandwiches in it such that no two classic sandwiches are touching each other. Now keep the fryer at 250 degrees for around 15 minutes. Turn the classic sandwiches in between the cooking process to cook both slices. Serve the classic sandwiches with tomato ketchup or mint sauce.

Nutrition

Calories 232 |Fat 22 g |Protein 25 g |Sugar 5 g

131. Prawn Fried Baked Pastry

P Prep Time 15 m | P Cooking Time 35 m | 4 Servings

Ingredients

- 1 ½ cup all-purpose flour
- 2 tbsp. unsalted butter
- 2 green chilies that are finely chopped or mashed
- Add a lot of water to make the dough stiff and firm
- A pinch of salt to taste
- 1 lb. prawn
- ¼ cup boiled peas
- ½ tsp. cumin
- 1 tsp. coarsely crushed coriander
- 1 dry red chili broken into pieces
- A small amount of salt (to taste)
- ½ tsp. dried mango powder
- 1 tsp. powdered ginger
- ½ tsp. red chili powder
- 1-2 tbsp. coriander

Directions

1. You will first need to make the outer covering. In a large bowl, add the flour, butter, and enough water to knead it into the stiff dough. Transfer this to a container and leave it to rest for five minutes. Place a pan on medium flame and add the oil. Roast the mustard seeds and once roasted, add the coriander seeds and the chopped dry red chilies. Add all the dry ingredients for the filling and mix the ingredients well.

2. Add a little water and continue to mix the ingredients. Make small balls from the dough and wrap them. Cut the wrapped dough in half and spread a little water on the edges to help you

fold the halves into a cone. Add the filling to the cone and close the samosa. Preheat the Breville Smart Oven for about 5 to 6 minutes at 300 Fahrenheit. Place all the samosas in the frying pan and close the basket properly.

3.   Keep the Breville Smart Oven at 200 degrees for another 20 to 25 minutes. Around half point, open the basket and turn the samosas for even cooking. After that, fry at 250 degrees for about 10 minutes to give them the desired golden-brown color. Serve hot. Recommended sides are tamarind or mint sauce.

Nutrition

Calories 132 |Fat 1 g |Protein 15 g |Sugar 9 g

132. Fish Spicy Lemon Kebab

P Prep Time 10 m | P Cooking Time 25 m | 3 Servings

Ingredients

- 1 lb. boneless fish roughly chopped
- 3 onions chopped
- 5 green chilies-roughly chopped
- 1 ½ tbsp. ginger paste
- 1 ½ tsp garlic paste
- 1 ½ tsp salt
- 3 tsp lemon juice
- 2 tsp garam masala
- 4 tbsp. chopped coriander
- 3 tbsp. cream
- 2 tbsp. coriander powder
- 4 tbsp. fresh mint chopped
- 3 tbsp. chopped capsicum
- 3 eggs
- 2 ½ tbsp. white sesame seeds

Directions

1.   Take all the ingredients mentioned under the first heading and mix them in a bowl. Grind them thoroughly to make a smooth paste. Take the eggs in a different bowl and beat them. Add a pinch of salt and leave them aside. Take a flat plate and in it, mix the sesame seeds and breadcrumbs. Mold the mixture of fish into small balls and flatten them into round and flat kebabs. Dip these kebabs in the egg and salt mixture and then in the mixture of breadcrumbs and sesame seeds. Leave these kebabs in the fridge for an hour or so to set.

2.   Preheat the Breville smart oven at 160 degrees Fahrenheit for around 5 minutes. Place the kebabs in the basket and let them cook for another 25 minutes at the same temperature. Turn the kebabs over in between the cooking process to get a uniform cook. Serve the kebabs with mint sauce.

Nutrition

Calories 432 |Fat 3 g |Protein 22 g |Sugar 1 g

133. Fish Oregano Fingers

P Prep Time 10 m | P Cooking Time 25 m | 5 Servings

Ingredients

- ½ lb. firm white fish fillet cut into Oregano Fingers
- 1 tbsp. lemon juice
- 2 cups of dry breadcrumbs

- 1 cup oil for frying
- 1 ½ tbsp. ginger-garlic paste
- 3 tbsp. lemon juice
- 2 tsp salt
- 1 ½ tsp pepper powder
- 1 tsp red chili
- 3 eggs
- 5 tbsp. corn flour
- 2 tsp tomato ketchup

Directions

1.   Rub a little lemon juice on the oregano fingers and set aside. Wash the fish after an hour and pat dry. Make the marinade and transfer the oregano fingers into the marinade. Allow them to dry on a plate for fifteen minutes. Now cover the oregano fingers with the crumbs and set aside to dry for fifteen minutes.

2.   Preheat the Breville smart oven at 160 degrees Fahrenheit for 5 minutes or so. Keep the fish in the fry basket now and close it properly.

3.   Let the oregano fingers cook at the same temperature for another 25 minutes. In between the cooking process, toss the fish once in a while to avoid burning the food. Serve either with tomato ketchup or chili sauce. Mint sauce also works well with the fish.

Nutrition

Calories 234 |Fat 3 g |Protein 35 g |Sugar 0 g

134. Prawn Grandma's Easy to Cook Wontons

P Prep Time 5 m | P Cooking Time 20 m | 3 Servings

Ingredients

- 1 ½ cup all-purpose flour
- ½ tsp. salt
- 5 tbsp. water
- 2 cups minced prawn
- 2 tbsp. oil
- 2 tsp. ginger-garlic paste
- 2 tsp. soya sauce
- 2 tsp. vinegar

Directions

1.   Squeeze out the dough and cover it with plastic wrap and set it aside. Then cook the ingredients for the filling and try to make sure the shrimp are well coated with the sauce. Roll out the dough and place the filling in the center.

2.   Now, roll the dough to cover the filling and bring the edges together. Preheat the Breville Smart Oven to 200 ° F for 5 minutes. Place the wontons in the pan and close it. Let them cook at equal temperature for another 20 minutes. Recommended sides are chili sauce or ketchup.

Nutrition

Calories 423 |Fat 20 g |Protein 20 g |Sugar 2 g

135. Tuna Sandwich

P Prep Time 5 m | P Cooking Time 15 m | 4 Servings

Ingredients

- 2 slices of white bread

- 1 tbsp. softened butter
- 1 tin tuna
- 1 small capsicum
- For Barbeque Sauce:
- ¼ tbsp. Worcestershire sauce
- ½ tsp. olive oil
- ¼ tsp. mustard powder
- ½ flake garlic crushed
- ¼ cup chopped onion
- ½ tbsp. sugar
- 1 tbsp. tomato ketchup
- ½ cup water.
- ¼ tbsp. red chili sauce
- Salt and black pepper to taste

Directions

1.   Remove the edges of the slices of bread. Now cut the slices horizontally. Cook the ingredients for the sauce and wait till it thickens. Now, add the lamb to the sauce and stir till it obtains the flavors. Roast the capsicum and peel the skin off. Cut the capsicum into slices. Mix the ingredients and apply it to the bread slices.

2.   Pre-heat the Breville smart oven for 5 minutes at 300 Fahrenheit. Open the basket of the Fryer and place the prepared classic sandwiches in it such that no two classic sandwiches are touching each other. Now keep the fryer at 250 degrees for around 15 minutes. Turn the classic sandwiches in between the cooking process to cook both slices. Serve the classic sandwiches with tomato ketchup or mint sauce.

Nutrition

Calories 460 |Fat 1 g |Protein 11 g |Sugar 5 g

136. Scallops And Spring Veggies

P Prep Time 10 m | P Cooking Time 8 m | 4 Servings

Ingredients

- ½ pound (226.8g) asparagus, ends trimmed, cut into 2-inch pieces
- 1 cup sugar snap peas
- 1 pound (453.592g) sea scallops
- 1 tablespoon lemon juice
- 2 teaspoons olive oil
- ½ teaspoon dried thyme
- Pinch salt
- Freshly ground black pepper

Directions:

1.   Place the asparagus and sugar snap peas in the air fryer basket.

2.   Cook for 2 to 3 minutes or until the vegetables are just starting to get tender.

3.   Meanwhile, check the scallops for a small muscle attached to the side, and pull it off and discard.

4.   In a medium bowl, toss the scallops with the lemon juice, olive oil, thyme, salt, and pepper. Place into the air fryer oven basket on top of the vegetables.

5.   Steam for 5 to 7 minutes, tossing the basket once during cooking time, until the scallops are just firm when tested with your finger and are opaque in the center, and the vegetables are tender. Serve immediately.

Nutrition:
calories: 162; carbs:10g; fat: 4g; protein:22g; fiber:3g

137. Air Fryer Salmon Patties

P Prep Time 8 m | P Cooking Time 7 m | 4 Servings
Ingredients
- 1 tbsp. Olive oil
- 1 tbsp. Ghee
- ¼ tsp. Salt
- 1/8 tsp. Pepper
- 1 egg
- 1 c. Almond flour
- 1 can wild alaskan pink salmon

Directions:
1. Drain can of salmon into a bowl and keep liquid. Discard skin and bones.
2. Add salt, pepper, and egg to salmon, mixing well with hands to incorporate. Make patties.
3. Dredge in flour and remaining egg. If it seems dry, spoon reserved salmon liquid from the can onto patties.
4. Pour the patties into the oven rack/basket. Place the rack on the middle-shelf of the air fryer oven. Set temperature to 378°f, and set time to 7 minutes. Cook 7 minutes till golden, making sure to flip once during cooking process.

Nutrition:
calories: 437; carbs:55; fat: 12g; protein:24g; sugar:2g

138. Salmon Noodles

P Prep Time 5 m | P Cooking Time 16 m | 4 Servings
Ingredients
- 1 salmon fillet
- 1 tbsp teriyaki marinade
- 3 ½ ozs soba noodles, cooked and drained
- 10 ozs firm tofu
- 7 ozs mixed salad
- 1 cup broccoli
- Olive oil
- Salt and pepper to taste

Directions:
1. Season the salmon with salt and pepper to taste, then coat with the teriyaki marinate. Set aside for 15 minutes
2. Preheat the air fryer oven at 350 degrees, then cook the salmon for 8 minutes.
3. Whilst the air fryer is cooking the salmon, start slicing the tofu into small cubes.
4. Next, slice the broccoli into smaller chunks. Drizzle with olive oil.
5. Once the salmon is cooked, put the broccoli and tofu into the air fryer oven tray for 8 minutes.
6. Plate the salmon and broccoli tofu mixture over the soba noodles. Add the mixed salad to the side and serve.

139. Beer-battered fish and chips

P Prep Time 5 m | P Cooking Time 30 m | 4 Servings

Ingredients

- 2 eggs
- 1 cup malty beer, such as pabst blue ribbon
- 1 cup all-purpose flour
- ½ cup cornstarch
- 1 teaspoon garlic powder
- Salt
- Pepper
- Cooking oil
- (4-ounce) cod fillets

Directions:

1 In a medium bowl, beat the eggs with the beer. In another medium bowl, combine the flour and cornstarch, and season with the garlic powder and salt and pepper to taste.

2 Spray the air fryer basket with cooking oil.

3 Dip each cod fillet in the flour and cornstarch mixture and then in the egg and beer mixture. Dip the cod in the flour and cornstarch a second time.

4 Place the cod in the air fryer oven. Do not stack. Cook in batches. Spray with cooking oil. Cook for 8 minutes.

5 Open the air fryer oven and flip the cod. Cook for an additional 7 minutes.

6 Remove the cooked cod from the air fryer, then repeat steps 4 and 5 for the remaining fillets.

7 Serve with prepared air fried frozen fries. Frozen fries will need to be cooked for 18 to 20 minutes at 400ºf.

8 Cool before serving.

Nutrition:

calories: 325; carbs:41; fat: 4g; protein:26g; fiber:1g

140. Tuna Stuffed Potatoes

P Prep Time 5 m | P Cooking Time 30 m | 4 Servings

Ingredients

- 4 starchy potatoes
- ½ tablespoon olive oil
- 1 (6-ounce) can tuna, drained
- 2 tablespoons plain greek yogurt
- 1 teaspoon red chili powder
- Salt and freshly ground black pepper, to taste
- 1 scallion, chopped and divided
- 1 tablespoon capers

Directions:

- In a large bowl of water, soak the potatoes for about 30 minutes. Drain well and pat dry with paper towel.
- Preheat the air fryer to 355 degrees f. Place the potatoes in a fryer basket.
- Cook for about 30 minutes.
- Meanwhile in a bowl, add tuna, yogurt, red chili powder, salt, black pepper and half of scallion and with a potato masher, mash the mixture completely.
- Remove the potatoes from the air fryer oven and place onto a smooth surface.
- Carefully, cut each potato from top side lengthwise.
- With your fingers, press the open side of potato halves slightly. Stuff the potato open portion with tuna mixture evenly.

- Sprinkle with the capers and remaining scallion. Serve immediately.

Nutrition:
Calories: 795, Protein: 109.77g, Fat: g, Carbs: g

141. Fried Calamari

P Prep Time 8 m | P Cooking Time 7 m | 6-8 Servings

Ingredients
- ½ tsp. Salt
- ½ tsp. Old bay seasoning
- 1/3 c. Plain cornmeal
- ½ c. Semolina flour
- ½ c. Almond flour
- 5-6 c. Olive oil
- 1 ½ pounds (680.389g) baby squid

Directions:
1 Rinse squid in cold water and slice tentacles, keeping just ¼-inch of the hood in one piece.
2 Combine 1-2 pinches of pepper, salt, old bay seasoning, cornmeal, and both flours together. Dredge squid pieces into flour mixture and place into the air fryer basket.
3 Spray liberally with olive oil. Cook 15 minutes at 345 degrees till coating turns a golden brown.

Nutrition:
Calories: 211; carbs:55; fat: 6g; protein:21g; sugar:1g

142. Soy And Ginger Shrimp

P Prep Time 8 m | P Cooking Time 10 m | 4 Servings

Ingredients
- 2 tablespoons olive oil
- 2 tablespoons scallions, finely chopped
- 2 cloves garlic, chopped
- 1 teaspoon fresh ginger, grated
- 1 tablespoon dry white wine
- 1 tablespoon balsamic vinegar
- 1/4 cup soy sauce
- 1 tablespoon sugar
- 1 pound (453.592g) shrimp
- Salt and ground black pepper, to taste

Directions:
- To make the marinade, warm the oil in a saucepan; cook all ingredients, except the shrimp, salt, and black pepper. Now, let it cool.
- Marinate the shrimp, covered, at least an hour, in the refrigerator.
- After that, pour into the oven rack/basket. Place the rack on the middle-shelf of the air fryer oven. Set temperature to 350°f, and set time to 10 minutes. Bake the shrimp at 350 degrees f for 8 to 10 minutes (depending on the size), turning once or twice. Season prepared shrimp with salt and black pepper and serve.

Nutrition:
Calories: 233, Protein: 24.55g, Fat: 10.28g, Carbs: 10.86g

143. Crispy Cheesy Fish Fingers

P Prep Time 10 m | P Cooking Time 20 m | 4 Servings

Ingredients

- Large cod fish filet, approximately 6-8 ounces, fresh or frozen and thawed, cut into 1 ½-inch strips
- 2 raw eggs
- ½ cup of breadcrumbs (we like panko, but any brand or home recipe will do)
- 2 tablespoons of shredded or powdered parmesan cheese
- 1 tablespoons of shredded cheddar cheese
- Pinch of salt and pepper

Directions:

1 Cover the basket of the air fryer oven with a lining of tin foil, leaving the edges uncovered to allow air to circulate through the basket.

2 Preheat the air fryer oven to 350 degrees.

3 In a large mixing bowl, beat the eggs until fluffy and until the yolks and whites are fully combined.

4 Dunk all the fish strips in the beaten eggs, fully submerging.

5 In a separate mixing bowl, combine the bread crumbs with the parmesan, cheddar, and salt and pepper, until evenly mixed.

6 One by one, coat the egg-covered fish strips in the mixed dry ingredients so that they're fully covered, and place on the foil-lined air fryer basket.

7 Set the air fryer oven timer to 20 minutes.

8 Halfway through the cooking time, shake the handle of the air fryer so that the breaded fish jostles inside and fry coverage is even.

9 After 20 minutes, when the fryer shuts off, the fish strips will be perfectly cooked and their breaded crust golden-brown and delicious! Using tongs, remove from the air fryer and set on a serving dish to cool.

Nutrition:

Calories: 124, Protein: 6.86g, Fat: 5.93g, Carbs: 12.26g

VEGETABLES RECIPES

144. Crispy Brussels Sprouts

P Prep Time 5 m | P Cooking Time 10 m | 2 Servings

Ingredients:
- ½ pound brussels sprouts, cut in half
- ½ tablespoon oil
- ½ tablespoon unsalted butter, melted

Directions:
1. Rub sprouts with oil.
2. Place into the air fryer basket.
3. Cook at 400F for 10 minutes. Stir once at the halfway mark.
4. Remove the air fryer basket and drizzle with melted butter.
5. Serve.

Nutrition:
Calories: 90 Fat: 6.1g Carb: 4g Protein: 2.9g

145. Flatbread

P Prep Time 5 m | P Cooking Time 7 m | 2 Servings

Ingredients:
- 1 cup shredded mozzarella cheese
- ¼ cup almond flour
- 1-ounce full-fat cream cheese softened

Directions:
1. Melt mozzarella in the microwave for 30 seconds. Stir in almond flour until smooth.
2. Add cream cheese. Continue mixing until dough forms. Knead with wet hands if necessary.
3. Divide the dough into two pieces and roll out to ¼-inch thickness between two pieces of parchment.
4. Cover the air fryer basket with parchment and place the flatbreads into the air fryer basket. Work in batches if necessary.
5. Cook at 320F for 7 minutes. Flip once at the halfway mark.
6. Serve.

Nutrition:
Calories: 296 Fat: 22.6g Carb: 3.3g Protein: 16.3g

146. Creamy Cabbage

P Prep Time 10 m | P Cooking Time 20 m | 2 Servings

Ingredients:
- ½ green cabbage head, chopped
- ½ yellow onion, chopped
- Salt and black pepper, to taste
- ½ cup whipped cream
- 1 tablespoon cornstarch

Directions:
1. Put cabbage and onion in the air fryer.
2. In a bowl, mix cornstarch with cream, salt, and pepper. Stir and pour over cabbage.
3. Toss and cook at 400F for 20 minutes.

4.   Serve.
Nutrition:
Calories: 208 Fat: 10g Carb: 16g Protein: 5g

147. Creamy Potatoes

P Prep Time 10 m | P Cooking Time 20 m | 2 Servings
Ingredients:
- ¾ pound potatoes, peeled and cubed
- 1 tablespoon olive oil
- Salt and black pepper, to taste
- ½ tablespoon hot paprika
- ½ cup Greek yogurt

Directions:
1.   Place potatoes in a bowl, pour water to cover, and leave aside for 10 minutes. Drain, pat dry, then transfer to another bowl.
2.   Add salt, pepper, paprika, and half of the oil to the potatoes and mix.
3.   Put potatoes in the air fryer basket and cook at 360F for 20 minutes.
4.   In a bowl, mix yogurt with salt, pepper, and the rest of the oil and whisk.
5.   Divide potatoes onto plates, drizzle with yogurt dressing, mix, and serve.
Nutrition:
Calories: 170 Fat: 3g Carb: 20g Protein: 5g

148. Green Beans And Cherry Tomatoes

P Prep Time 10 m | P Cooking Time 15 m | 2 Servings
Ingredients:
- 8 ounces cherry tomatoes
- 8 ounces green beans
- 1 tablespoon olive oil
- Salt and black pepper, to taste

Directions:
1.   In a bowl, mix cherry tomatoes with green beans, olive oil, salt, and pepper. Mix.
2.   Cook in the air fryer at 400 degrees F for 15 minutes. Shake once.
3.   Serve.
Nutrition:
Calories: 162 Fat: 6g Carb: 8g Protein: 9g

149. Crispy Brussels Sprouts And Potatoes

P Prep Time 10 m | P Cooking Time 8 m | 2 Servings
Ingredients:
- ¾ pound brussels sprouts, washed and trimmed
- ½ cup new potatoes, chopped
- 2 teaspoons bread crumbs
- Salt and black pepper, to taste
- 2 teaspoons butter

Directions:
1.   In a bowl, add Brussels sprouts, potatoes, bread crumbs, salt, pepper, and butter. Mix well.
2.   Place in the air fryer and cook at 400F for 8 minutes.

3.   Serve.
Nutrition:
Calories: 152 Fat: 3g Carb: 17g Protein: 4g

150. Herbed Tomatoes

P Prep Time 10 m | P Cooking Time 15 m | 2 Servings
Ingredients:
- 2 big tomatoes, halved and insides scooped out
- Salt and black pepper, to taste
- ½ tablespoon olive oil
- 1 clove garlic, minced
- ¼ teaspoon thyme, chopped

Directions:
1.   In the air fryer, mix tomatoes with thyme, garlic, oil, salt, and pepper.
2.   Mix and cook at 390F for 15 minutes.
3.   Serve.
Nutrition:
Calories: 112 Fat: 1g Carb: 4g Protein: 4g

151. Air Fried Leeks

P Prep Time 10 m | P Cooking Time 7 m | 2 Servings
Ingredients:
- 2 leeks, washed, ends cut, and halved
- Salt and black pepper, to taste
- ½ tablespoon butter, melted
- ½ tablespoon lemon juice

Directions:
1.   Rub leeks with melted butter and season with salt and pepper.
2.   Lay it inside the air fryer and cook at 350F for 7 minutes.
3.   Arrange on a platter. Drizzle with lemon juice and serve.
Nutrition:
Calories: 100 Fat: 4g Carb: 6g Protein: 2g

152. Crispy Broccoli

P Prep Time 10 m | P Cooking Time 10 m | 4 Servings
Ingredients:
- 1 large head fresh broccoli
- 2 teaspoons olive oil
- tablespoon lemon juice

Directions:
1.   Rinse the broccoli and pat dry. Cut off the florets and separate them. You can also use the broccoli stems too; cut them into 1" chunks and peel them.
2.   Toss the broccoli, olive oil, and lemon juice in a large bowl until coated.
3.   Roast the broccoli in the air fryer, in batches, for 10 to 14 minutes or until the broccoli is crisp-tender and slightly brown around the edges. Repeat with the remaining broccoli. Serve immediately.
Nutrition:
Calories: 63; Fat: 2g Protein: 4g; Carbohydrates: 10g; Sodium: 50mg; Fiber: 4g;

153. Garlic-Roasted Bell Peppers

P Prep Time 5 m | P Cooking Time 20 m | 4 Servings

Ingredients:

- 4 bell peppers, any colors, stemmed, seeded, membranes removed, and cut into fourths
- 1 teaspoon olive oil
- 4 garlic cloves, minced
- ½ teaspoon dried thyme

Directions:

1. Put the peppers in the basket of the air fryer and drizzle with olive oil. Toss gently. Roast for 15 minutes.
2. Sprinkle with the garlic and thyme. Roast for 3 to 5 minutes more, or until tender. Serve immediately.

Nutrition:

Calories: 36; Fat: 1g Protein: 1g; Carbohydrates: 5g; Sodium: 21mg; Fiber: 2g;

154. Asparagus With Garlic

P Prep Time 5 m | P Cooking Time 10 m | 4 Servings

Ingredients:

- 1-pound asparagus, rinsed, ends snapped off where they naturally break (see Tip)
- 2 teaspoons olive oil
- 3 garlic cloves, minced
- 2 tablespoons balsamic vinegar
- ½ teaspoon dried thyme

Directions:

1. In a huge bowl, mix the asparagus with olive oil. -Transfer to the air fryer basket.
2. Sprinkle with garlic. Roast for 4 to 5 minutes for crisp-tender or for 8 to 11 minutes for asparagus that is crisp on the outside and tender on the inside.
3. Drizzle with the balsamic vinegar and sprinkle with the thyme leaves. Serve immediately.

Nutrition:

Calories: 41; Fat: 1g Protein: 3g; Carbohydrates: 6g; Sodium: 3mg;

155. Cheesy Roasted Sweet Potatoes

P Prep Time 5 m | P Cooking Time 20 m | 4 Servings

Ingredients:

- 2 large sweet potatoes, peeled and sliced
- 1 teaspoon olive oil
- 1 tablespoon white balsamic vinegar
- 1 teaspoon dried thyme
- ¼ cup grated Parmesan cheese

Directions:

1. In a big bowl, shower the sweet potato slices with the olive oil and toss.
2. Sprinkle with the balsamic vinegar and thyme and toss again.
3. Sprinkle the potatoes with the Parmesan cheese and toss to coat.
4. Roast the slices, in batches, in the air fryer basket for 18 to 23 minutes, tossing the sweet potato slices in the basket once during cooking, until tender.
5. Repeat with the remaining sweet potato slices. Serve immediately.

Nutrition:

156. Mushroom and Feta Frittata

P Prep Time 5 m | P Cooking Time 30 m | 4 Servings

Ingredients:
- cups button mushrooms
- red onion
- tablespoons olive oil
- tablespoons feta cheese, crumbled
- Pinch of salt
- eggs
- Cooking spray

Directions:

1 Add olive oil to pan and sauté mushrooms over medium heat until tender. Remove from heat and pan so that they can cool. Preheat your air fryer to 330 degree F.

2 Add cracked eggs into a bowl, and whisk them, adding a pinch of salt. Coat an 8-inch heat resistant baking dish with cooking spray. Add the eggs into the baking dish, then onion and mushroom mixture, and then add feta cheese.

3 Place the baking dish into air fryer for 30-minutes and serve warm.

Nutrition:

Calories: 246 kcal| Total Fat: 12.3 g | Carbohydrates: 9.2 g | Protein: 10.3 g

157. Cauliflower pizza crust

P Prep Time 26 m | P Cooking Time 20 m | 4 Servings

Ingredients:
- 1 (12-oz.) Steamer bag cauliflower
- 1 large egg.
- ½ cup shredded sharp cheddar cheese.
- tbsp. Blanched finely ground almond flour
- 1 tsp. Italian blend seasoning

Directions:

1 Cook cauliflower according to package instructions. Remove from bag and place into cheesecloth or paper towel to remove excess water. Place cauliflower into a large bowl.

2 Cut a piece of parchment to fit your air fryer basket. Press cauliflower into 6-inch round circle. Place into the air fryer basket. Adjust the temperature to 360°F and set the timer for 11 minutes. After 7 minutes, flip the pizza crust

3 Add preferred toppings to pizza. Place back into air fryer basket and cook for an additional 4 minutes or until fully cooked and golden. Serve right away.

Nutrition:

Calories: 230 kcal| Protein: 14.9 g |Fiber: 4.7 g | Fat: 14.2 g | Carbohydrates: 10.0 g

158. Olives and artichokes

P Prep Time 20 m | P Cooking Time 15 m | 4 Servings

Ingredients:
- oz. canned artichoke hearts, drained
- ½ cup tomato sauce
- cups black olives, pitted
- garlic cloves; minced
- 1 tbsp. Olive oil
- 1 tsp. Garlic powder

Directions:

1 In a pan that fits your air fryer, mix the olives with the artichokes and the other ingredients, toss,

2 put the pan in the fryer and cook at 350°f for 15 minutes

Divide the mix between plates and serve.

Nutrition:

Calories: 180 kcal |Fat: 4 g |Fiber: 3 g | Carbohydrates: 5 g | Protein: 6 g

159. Lemon asparagus

P Prep Time 17 m | P Cooking Time 12 m | 4 Servings

Ingredients:

- 1 lb. Asparagus, trimmed
- garlic cloves; minced
- tbsp. Parmesan, grated
- tbsp. Olive oil
- Juice of 1 lemon
- A pinch of salt and black pepper

Directions:

1 Take a bowl and mix the asparagus with the rest of the ingredients and toss.

2 Put the asparagus in your air fryer's basket and cook at 390°F for 12 minutes. Divide between plates and serve!

Nutrition:

Calories: 175 kcal |Fat: 5 g |Fiber: 2 g | Carbohydrates: 4 g| Protein: 8 g

160. Savory cabbage and tomatoes

P Prep Time 20 m | P Cooking Time 15 m | 4 Servings

Ingredients:

- Spring onions; chopped.
- 1 savoy cabbage, shredded
- 1 tbsp. Parsley; chopped.
- tbsp. Tomato sauce
- Salt and black pepper to taste.

Directions:

1 In a pan that fits your air fryer, mix the cabbage the rest of the ingredients except the parsley, toss, put the pan in the fryer and cook at 360°f for 15 minutes

2 Divide between plates and serve with parsley sprinkled on top.

Nutrition:

Calories: 163 kcal| Fat: 4 g | Fiber: 3 g | Carbohydrates: 6 g| Protein: 7 g

161. Pecan brownies

P Prep Time 30 m | P Cooking Time 20 m | 6 Servings

Ingredients:

- ¼ cup chopped pecans
- ¼ cup low carb
- Sugar: -free chocolate chips.
- ¼ cup unsalted butter; softened.
- 1 large egg.
- ½ cup blanched finely ground almond flour.

- ½ cup powdered erythritol
- tbsp. Unsweetened cocoa powder
- ½ tsp. Baking powder.

Directions:

1 Take a large bowl, mix almond flour, erythritol, cocoa powder and baking powder. Stir in butter and egg.

2 Adjust the temperature to 300°F and set the timer for 20 minutes. When fully cooked a toothpick inserted in center will come out clean. Allow 20 minutes to fully cool and firm up.

Nutrition:

Calories: 215 kcal| Protein: 4.2 g |Fiber: 2.8 g | Fat: 18.9 g | Carbohydrates: 21.8 g

162. Cheesy endives

P Prep Time 20 m | P Cooking Time 15 m | 4 Servings

Ingredients:

- endives, trimmed
- ¼ cup goat cheese, crumbled
- 1 tbsp. Lemon juice
- Tbsp. Chives; chopped.
- tbsp. Olive oil
- 1 tsp. Lemon zest, grated
- A pinch of salt and black pepper

Directions:

1 Take a bowl and mix the endives with the other ingredients except the cheese and chives and toss well.

2 Put the endives in your air fryer's basket and cook at 380°F for 15 minutes

3 Divide the corn between plates.

4 Serve with cheese and chives sprinkled on top.

Nutrition:

Calories: 140 kcal |Fat: 4 g | Fiber: 3 g | Carbohydrates: 5 g| Protein: 7 g

163. Cauliflower steak

P Prep Time 12 m | P Cooking Time 7 m | 4 Servings

Ingredients:

- 1 medium head cauliflower
- ¼ cup blue cheese crumbles
- ¼ cup hot sauce
- ¼ cup full-fat ranch dressing
- Tbsp. Salted butter; melted.

Directions:

1 Remove cauliflower leaves. Slice the head in ½-inch-thick slices.

2 In a small bowl, mix hot sauce and butter. Brush the mixture over the cauliflower.

3 Place each cauliflower steak into the air fryer, working in batches if necessary. Adjust the temperature to 400°F and set the timer for 7 minutes

4 When cooked, edges will begin turning dark and caramelized. To serve, sprinkle steaks with crumbled blue cheese. Drizzle with ranch dressing.

Nutrition:

Calories: 122 kcal |Protein: 4.9 g | Fiber: 3.0 g| Fat: 8.4 g | Carbohydrates: 7.7 g

164. Parmesan Broccoli and Asparagus

P Prep Time 20 m | P Cooking Time 15 m | 4 Servings
Ingredients:
- ½ lb. asparagus, trimmed
- 1 broccoli head, florets separated
- Juice of 1 lime
- tbsp. parmesan, grated
- tbsp. olive oil
- Salt and black pepper to taste.

Directions:
1 Take a bowl and mix the asparagus with the broccoli and all the other ingredients except the parmesan, toss, transfer to your air fryer's basket and cook at 400°F for 15 minutes
2 Divide between plates, sprinkle the parmesan on top and serve.

Nutrition:
Calories: 172 kcal |Fat: 5 g | Fiber: 2 g |Carbohydrates: 4 g | Protein: 9 g

165. Air Fryer Crunchy Cauliflower

P Prep Time 20 m | P Cooking Time 15 m | 5 Servings
Ingredients:
- oz. cauliflower
- 1 tbsp. potato starch
- 1 tsp. olive oil
- Salt & pepper to taste

Directions:
1. Set the air fryer toaster oven to 400°F and preheat it for 3 minutes. Slice cauliflower into equal pieces and if you are using potato starch then toss with the florets into bowl.
2. Add some olive oil and mix to coat.
3. Use olive oil cooking spray for spraying the inside of air fryer toaster oven basket then add cauliflower.
4. Cook for eight minutes then shake the basket and cook for another 5 minutes depending on your desired level of crisp. Sprinkle roasted cauliflower with fresh parsley, kosher salt, and your seasonings or sauce of your choice.

Nutrition:
Calories: 36 kcal |Fat: 1 g |Protein: 1 g |Carbs: 5 g | Fiber: 2 g

166. Air Fryer Veg Buffalo Cauliflower

P Prep Time 20 m | P Cooking Time 15 m | 3 Servings
Ingredients:
- 1 medium head cauliflower
- tsp. avocado oil
- tbsp. red hot sauce
- tbsp. nutritional yeast
- 1 1/2 tsp. maple syrup
- 1/4 tsp. sea salt
- 1 tbsp. cornstarch or arrowroot starch

Directions:
1 Set your air fryer toaster oven to 360°F. Place all the ingredients to bowl except cauliflower. Mix them to combine.

2 Put the cauliflower and mix to coat equally. Put half of your cauliflower to air fryer and cook for 15 minutes but keep shaking them until your get desired consistency.

3Do the same for the cauliflower which is left except lower Cooking Time to 10 minutes.

4 Keep the cauliflower tightly sealed in refrigerator for 3-4 days. For heating again add back to air fryer for 1-2 minutes until crispness.

Nutrition:

Calories: 248 kcal |Fat: 20g |Protein: 4g| Carbs: 13g| Fiber: 2g

167. Air Fryer Asparagus

P Prep Time 5 m | P Cooking Time 13 m | 2 Servings

Ingredients:

- Nutritional yeast
- Olive oil nonstick spray
- One bunch of asparagus

Directions:

1 Wash asparagus and then trim off thick, woody ends.

2 Spray asparagus with olive oil spray and sprinkle with yeast.

3 Add the asparagus to air fryer rack/basket in a singular layer. Set temperature to 360°F and set time to 8 minutes. Select START/STOP to begin.

Nutrition:

Calories: 17 kcal |Total Fat: 8 g| Total Carbs: 2 g| Protein: 9 g

168. Almond Flour Battered and Crisped Onion Rings

P Prep Time 5 m | P Cooking Time 20 m | 3 Servings

Ingredients:

- ½ cup almond flour
- ¾ cup coconut milk
- 1 big white onion, sliced into rings
- 1 egg, beaten
- 1 tablespoon baking powder
- 1 tablespoon smoked paprika
- Salt and pepper to taste

Directions:

1 Preheat the air fryer Oven for 5 minutes.

2 In a mixing bowl, mix the almond flour, baking powder, smoked paprika, salt and pepper.

3 In another bowl, combine the eggs and coconut milk.

4 Soak the onion slices into the egg mixture.

5 Dredge the onion slices in the almond flour mixture.

6 Pour into the Oven rack/basket. Set temperature to 325°F and set time to 15 minutes. Select START/STOP to begin. Shake the fryer basket for even cooking.

Nutrition:

Calories: 217 kcal |Total Fat: 17 g | Total Carbs: 2 g | Fiber: 6 g | Protein: 5 g

169. Air Fryer Buffalo Cauliflower

P Prep Time 5 m | P Cooking Time 13 m | 6 Servings

Ingredients

- 2 medium head Cauliflowers which should be carefully chopped to florets that can be eaten in one scoop

- 4-6 tablespoons of red hot spice/sauce.
- ½ teaspoon of salt
- 2 tablespoon of arrowroot starch. You can also use cornstarch
- 3 teaspoons of maple syrup
- 4 spoons of your favorite avocado oil
- 4 tablespoons of nutritional yeast

Directions
1. First of all, make sure to cook with your Air Fryer at 360F.
2. Then add all your ingredients to a large bowl except the cauliflower.
3. Whisk the ingredients in the bowl until it is thorough.
4. Add the cauliflower and toss it to coat evenly.
5. Proceed to add half of your cauliflower to your new Air Fryer.
6. Cook for about 13 minutes and you can shake halfway through the cooking process.
7. If you have leftovers, then you can reheat in your Air Fryer for about 2 minutes.

Nutrition
Calories 118 |Fat 5 g |Protein 31 g |Sugar 5 g

170. Air Fryer Kale Chips

P Prep Time 5 m | P Cooking Time 5 m | 2 Servings
Ingredients
- 1½ bunch of kale
- 1½ tbsp. oil
- Salt (to taste, preferably a pinch)
- Seasonings (as flavor): ranch or any of your choice

Directions
1. Wash kale under running water and dry.
2. Cut out the leaves and then, into small pieces into a bowl.
3. Pour oil into them and rub it vigorously into the leaves such that every piece is coated with oil.
4. Add salt, shaking the bowl sideways to make sure they are coated well.
5. Arrange kale into the air fryer basket while preventing overlapping and curling of leaves. Don't forget to cook them in batches if they cannot all fit into the basket at once.
6. Preheat the air fryer to 375ºF.
7. Set the timer to 3-5 minutes and cook until they are crispy. So that they cook evenly, ensure you shake the basket at least once during cooking.
8. Serve warm while sprinkling the seasoning minimally as flavor to your kale chips.

Nutrition
Calories 345 |Fat 9 g |Protein 27 g |Sugar 7 g

171. Air Fried Mozzarella Stalks

P Prep Time 5 m | P Cooking Time 10 m | 6 Servings
Ingredients
- 15 mozzarella sticks: cut from a block of cheese
- ½ cup general-purpose flour
- 2 Eggs
- 1½ cups breadcrumbs
- Spices: onion powder, garlic powder, smoked paprika (1 tsp. each) and salt (to taste).
- Sauce: any of your choice but for this book, we'll be using marinara

Directions
1.   Make your mozzarella sticks by cutting them straight from cheese blocks (you may have them pre-cut though).
2.   Arrange cheese sticks on a plate (parchment-lined for ease) and freeze in a freezer for about 40 minutes to prevent melting when placed into the air fryer.
3.   You may seize your flour to remove air bubbles and place inside a covered bowl.
4.   Break eggs and whisk well in a bowl.
5.   Pour and mix spices and breadcrumb into a bowl.
6.   Coat the mozzarella sticks evenly by placing them into the covered bowl or container, cover tightly, and shake. Open the bowl, take out the sticks one at a time, place into the whisked egg, and then into the mixture of the spices and crumbs.
7.   Place the coated sticks back on the plate and freeze for about 30 minutes more this time around.
8.   Get your air fryer out and clean it (you can do that before the whole cooking process though).
9.   Grease the air fryer racks lightly.
10.   Preheat the air fryer to 390ºF.
11.   Take out the mozzarella sticks from the freezer and once more, place into the whisked egg, and then into the mixture of the spices and crumbs. Once you are done, transfer them to the air fryer in batches if they cannot all fit into the rack.
12.   Set the timer to 7-10 minutes and cook until you have crispy, golden brown mozzarella sticks.
13.   Serve with marinara or any sauce of your choice.

Nutrition
Calories 113 |Fat 11 g |Protein 36 g |Sugar 2 g

172. Air Fryer Vegan Fried Ravioli

P Prep Time 5 m | P Cooking Time 10 m | 2 Servings

Ingredients
- ¼ cup of Panko bread crumbs
- ½ teaspoons of dried basil
- 1 teaspoon of your favorite nutritional yeast flakes
- Pinch of pepper and small salt to taste
- ¼ cup of aquafaba liquid from the can or you can use other beans
- ½ teaspoon of garlic powder
- ½ teaspoon of dried oregano
- ¼ cup of marinara to dip
- 4 ounces of thawed vegan ravioli

Directions
1.   Combine the nutritional yeast flakes, dried oregano, salt, pepper, dried basil, garlic powder, and panko bread crumbs on a plate or a clean surface.
2.   Put your aquafaba in a separate bowl.
3.   Carefully dip the ravioli in the aquafaba, and shake off the excess liquid.
4.   After that, dredge it in the bread crumbs mixture while making sure that your ravioli is well covered.
5.   Then, move the ravioli into the air fryer basket.
6.   Do these steps for all the ravioli you want to cook.

7.   Make sure to space the ravioli well in the air fryer basket to ensure that they can turn brown evenly.
8.   Then go on to spritz your ravioli with cooking spray in the air fryer basket.
9.   Set your air fryer to 390F.
10.   Cook for 7 minutes and carefully turn each ravioli on their sides. Try as much as possible not to shake the baskets as you will waste the bread crumbs. After turning, proceed to cook for 2 more minutes.
11.   Your ravioli is ready to eat. Make sure to serve with warm marinara as a dipping.
12.   Save your leftovers in the refrigerator and reheat when you are ready to eat.

Nutrition

Calories 321 |Fat 2 g |Protein 15 g | Sugar 4 g

173. Air Fryer Veg Pizza

P Prep Time 10 m | P Cooking Time 10 m | 4 Servings

Ingredients

*   Pizza
*   Pizza sauce
*   Olives (or other veg toppings of your choice)
*   Cheese
*   Basil
*   Pepper flakes

Directions

1.   If you are just fetching the pizza out of the freezer, you might want to warm it. Set the air fryer to 350ºF.
2.   Once warm, top the pizza with the pizza sauce.
3.   Add cheese to the pizza.
4.   Add olives to the pizza.
5.   Arrange the pizza carefully on the air fryer rack.
(NOTE: you can also set your dough into the air fryer rack before adding the toppings to prevent spills)
6.   Preheat the air fryer to 350ºF and spray air fryer rack with oil.
7.   Set the timer to 5-7 minutes and cook until the cheese is melted.
8.   Once cooked, let the cheese set on pizza by waiting for about 2-3 minutes before cutting.
9.   Serve warm while topping it with basil and pepper flakes.

Nutrition

Calories 409 |Fat 18 g |Protein 13 g |Sugar 8 g

174. Air Fryer Buffalo Cauliflower – Onion Dip

P Prep Time 10 m | P Cooking Time 12 m | 2 Servings

Ingredients

*   ¾ head of cauliflower
*   ¾ cup of buffalo sauce
*   Seasoning and spice: garlic powder (1½ tsp.) and salt (to taste)
*   Creamy dipping sauce: French onion dip (or any sauce of your choice)
*   Celery
*   3 tbsp. olive oil

Directions

1.   Cut the head of cauliflower into tiny florets into a big bowl.

2.   Add and mix the cauliflower with the buffalo sauce and the rest of the ingredients apart from the dip sauce and celery sticks.
3.   Grease the air fryer rack lightly.
4.   Preheat the air fryer to 375ºF.
5.   Transfer the well-mixed cauliflower to the air fryer in batches if they cannot all fit into the rack.
6.   Set the timer to 10-12 minutes and cook until the cauliflower florets are tender and browned a bit.
7.   Serve warm with the celery sticks and dipping sauce of your choice. In my case, french onion dip.

Nutrition
Calories 265 |Fat 6 g |Protein 20 g |Sugar 6 g

APPETIZERS RECIPES

175. Steamed Pot Stickers

P Prep Time 10 m | P Cooking Time 20 m | 30 Servings

Ingredients:

- ½ cup finely chopped cabbage
- 2 teaspoons low-sodium soy sauce
- 2 tablespoons cocktail sauce
- 30 wonton wrappers
- ¼ cup finely chopped red bell pepper
- 3 tablespoons water, and more for brushing the wrappers
- 2 green onions, finely chopped
- 1 egg, beaten

Directions:

1.   Combine the cabbage, bell pepper, chives, egg, cocktail sauce in a small bowl, and soy sauce and mix well.
2.   Put exactly 1 teaspoon of the mixture in the middle of each wonton wrapper. Fold the wrap in half, covering the filling. Wet the edges with water and seal. You can fold the edges of the wrapper with your fingers so they look like the stickers you get at restaurants. Brush them with water.
3.   Put 3 tablespoons of water in the skillet under the fryer basket. Cook pot stickers in 2 batches for 9 to 10 minutes or until pot stickers are hot and bottom is light.
4.   Substitution Tip: Use other veggies in this recipe, like chopped corn, peas, or zucchini or squash in the summer. You can also add the rest of the cooked meat, such as minced pork or chicken.

Nutrition:

Calories: 291| Fat 2g| Cholesterol 35mg| Sodium 649mg| Carbo 57g |Fiber 3g |Protein 10g

176. Beef and Mango Skewers

P Prep Time 10 m | P Cooking Time 5 m | 4 Servings

Ingredients:

- 2 tablespoons balsamic vinegar
- 1 tablespoon olive oil
- 1 tablespoon honey
- ½ teaspoon dried marjoram
- Pinch salt
- Freshly ground black pepper
- 1 mango
- ¾ pound beef sirloin (cut into 1-inch cubes)

Directions:

1.   Put the meat cubes in a medium bowl and add the balsamic vinegar, olive oil, honey, marjoram, salt and pepper. Mix well and then massage the marinade into the meat with your hands. Set aside.
2.   To prepare the mango, leave it last and cut the skin with a sharp blade.
3.   Then gently cut around the oval pit to remove the pulp. Cut the mango into 1-inch cubes.
4.   The metal wire skewers alternate with three cubes of meat and two cubes of mango.
5.   Bake the skewers in the skillet for 4 to 7 minutes or until the meat is browned and at least 145 ° F.

Nutrition:
Calories 242|Fat 9g| Cholesterol 76mg |Sodium 96mg| Carbo 13g| Fiber 1g |Protein 26g

177. Curried Sweet Potato Fries

P Prep Time 5 m | P Cooking Time 12 m | 4 Servings
Ingredients:
- ½ cup sour cream
- ½ cup mango chutney
- 3 teaspoons curry powder, divided
- 4 cups frozen sweet potato fries
- 1 tablespoon olive oil
- Pinch salt
- Freshly ground black pepper

Directions:
1.   In a bowl, add together sour cream, chutney, and 1½ teaspoon curry powder. Mix well and let stand.
2.   Place the sweet potatoes in a sizeable bowl. Pour over the olive oil and sprinkle with the remaining 1½ teaspoon curry powder, salt, and pepper.
3.   Put the potatoes in the fryer basket. Cook 8 to 12 minutes or until crisp, hot and golden, shaking the basket once during cooking.
4.   Place the potatoes in a basket and serve with the teaspoon.
5.   Substitution Tip: You can choose to use fresh sweet potatoes instead of frozen potatoes. Take one or two sweet potatoes, peel them, and cut them into 1-inch-thick strips with a sharp knife or mandolin. Use according to the recipe instructions. But you will need to increase the time for cooking.
Nutrition:
Calories: 323| Fat 10g| Cholesterol: 13mg |Sodium: 138mg| Carbo 58g |Fiber: 7g |Protein: 3g

178. Spicy Kale Chips with Yogurt Sauce

P Prep Time 10 m | P Cooking Time 5 m | 4 Servings
Ingredients:
- 1 cup Greek yogurt
- 3 tablespoons lemon juice
- 2 tablespoons honey mustard
- ½ teaspoon dried oregano
- 1 bunch curly kale
- 2 tablespoons olive oil
- ½ teaspoon salt
- 1/2 teaspoon pepper

Directions:
1.   In a bowl, add together the yogurt, lemon juice, honey mustard, and oregano and set aside. \
2.   Remove the stems and ribs from the cabbage with a sharp knife. Cut the leaves into 2 to 3-inch pieces.
3.   Toss the cabbage with olive oil, salt, and pepper. Massage the oil with your hands.
4.   Fry the kale in batches until crisp, about 5 minutes, shaking the basket once during cooking. Serve with yogurt sauce.

5.	Ingredient Tip: Kale is available in different varieties. Tuscan (also known as dinosaur or lacing) is the most powerful and makes excellent marks. Kale, the variety widely found in grocery stores, can be slightly frozen when cooked in the deep fryer, but it's still delicious.
Nutrition:
Calories: 154| Fat: 8g |Cholesterol: 3mg| Sodium: 378mg |Carbo 13g |Fiber: 1g |Protein: 8g

179. Phyllo Artichoke Triangles

P Prep Time 15 m | P Cooking Time 9 m | 18 Servings
Ingredients:
- ¼ cup ricotta cheese
- 1 egg white
- 1/3 cup minced drained artichoke hearts
- 3 tablespoons grated mozzarella cheese
- ½ teaspoon dried thyme
- 6 sheets frozen phyllo dough, thawed
- 2 tablespoons melted butter

Directions:
1.	In a bowl, combine ricotta cheese, egg white, artichoke hearts, mozzarella cheese, and thyme and mix well.
2.	Cover the dough with a damp kitchen towel while you work so it doesn't dry out. Using one sheet at a time, lay it out on your work surface and cut into thirds lengthwise.
3.	Apply 1½ tsp of filling on each strip at the base. Fold the bottom right edge of the sheet over the filling to meet the other side in a triangle, then continue folding into a triangle. Brush each angle with butter to seal the edges. Repeat with the remaining dough and filling.
4.	Bake, 7 at a time, for about 3 to 4 minutes or until the sex is golden and crisp.
5.	Replacement Tip: You can use anything in this filling in place of artichoke hearts. Try spinach, minced shrimp, and cooked sausage or keep vegetarian and use all the grated cheese.
Nutrition:
Calories: 271 |Fat: 17g |Cholesterol: 19mg| Sodium: 232mg |Carbo 23g |Fiber: 5g| Protein: 9g

180. Arancini

P Prep Time 15 m | P Cooking Time 22 m | 16 Servings
Ingredients:
- 2 eggs, beaten
- 1½ cups panko bread crumbs, divided
- ½ cup grated Parmesan cheese
- 2 tablespoons minced fresh basil
- 2 cups cooked rice or leftover risotto
- 16 ¾-inch cubes mozzarella cheese
- 2 tablespoons olive oil

Directions:
1.	In a medium bowl, add together the rice, eggs, and a cup of breadcrumbs, Parmesan, and basil. Shape this mixture into 16 1-inch balls.
2.	Create a hole in each of the balls with your finger and place a cube of mozzarella. Glue the rice mixture firmly around the cheese.
3.	On a shallow plate, add together the remaining 1 cup of breadcrumbs with the olive oil and mix well. Wrap the rice balls in the breadcrumbs for color.
4.	Cook the rank in batches for 8 to 11 minutes or until golden brown.

5.   You knew that? In Italy, arancini, also called frittata or rice soup, is sold on the street as a snack. They have grown much larger in this country, the size of an orange, and are often cone-shaped.

Nutrition:

Calories: 378| Fat: 11g| Cholesterol: 57mg| Sodium: 361mg |Carbo 53g| Fiber: 2g |Protein: 16g

181. Steamed Pot Stickers

P Prep Time 20 m | P Cooking Time 10 m | 30 Servings

Ingredients

- ½ cup finely chopped cabbage
- 2 teaspoons low-sodium soy sauce
- 2 tablespoons cocktail sauce
- 30 wonton wrappers
- ¼ cup finely chopped red bell pepper
- 3 tablespoons water, and more for brushing the wrappers
- 2 green onions, finely chopped
- 1 egg, beaten

Directions

1.   Combine the cabbage, bell pepper, chives, egg, cocktail sauce in a small bowl, and soy sauce and mix well.

2.   Put exactly 1 teaspoon of the mixture in the middle of each wonton wrapper. Fold the wrap in half, covering the filling. wet the edges with water and seal. You can fold the edges of the wrapper with your fingers so they look like the stickers you get at restaurants. Brush them with water.

3.   Put 3 tablespoons of water in the skillet under the fryer basket. Cook potstickers in 2 batches for 9 to 10 minutes or until potstickers are hot and the bottom is light.

4.   Substitution Tip: Use other veggies in this recipe, like chopped corn, peas, or zucchini, or squash in the summer. You can also add the rest of the cooked meat, such as minced pork or chicken.

Nutrition

Calories 291 |Fat 2g |Saturated Fat 0g |Cholesterol 35mg |Sodium 649mg |Carbohydrates 57g |Fiber 3g |Protein 10g

182. Beef and Mango Skewers

P Prep Time 10 m | P Cooking Time 5 m | 4 Servings

Ingredients

- 2 tablespoons balsamic vinegar
- 1 tablespoon olive oil
- 1 tablespoon honey
- ½ teaspoon dried marjoram
- A pinch of salt
- Freshly ground black pepper
- 1 mango
- ¾ pound beef sirloin (cut into 1-inch cubes)

Directions

1.   Put the meat cubes in a medium bowl and add the balsamic vinegar, olive oil, honey, marjoram, salt, and pepper. Mix well and then massage the marinade into the meat with your hands. Set aside.

2.   To prepare the mango, leave it last and cut the skin with a sharp blade.
3.   Then gently cut around the oval pit to remove the pulp. Cut the mango into 1-inch cubes.
4.   The metal wire skewers alternate with three cubes of meat and two cubes of mango.
5.   Bake the skewers in the skillet for 4 to 7 minutes or until the meat is browned and at least 145 ° F.

Nutrition

Calories 242 |Fat 9g |Saturated Fat 3g|Cholesterol 76mg|Sodium 96mg|Carbohydrates 13g|Fiber 1g |Protein 26g

183. Curried Sweet Potato Fries

P Prep Time 5 m | P Cooking Time 12 m | 4 Servings

Ingredients

- ½ cup sour cream
- ½ cup mango chutney
- 3 teaspoons curry powder, divided
- 4 cups frozen sweet potato fries
- 1 tablespoon olive oil
- A pinch of salt
- Freshly ground black pepper

Directions

1.   In a bowl, add together sour cream, chutney, and 1½ teaspoon curry powder. Mix well and let stand.
2.   Place the sweet potatoes in a sizeable bowl. Pour over the olive oil and sprinkle with the remaining 1½ teaspoon curry powder, salt, and pepper.
3.   Put the potatoes in the fryer basket. Cook 8 to 12 minutes or until crisp, hot and golden, shaking the basket once during cooking.
4.   Place the potatoes in a basket and serve with the teaspoon.
5.   Substitution Tip: You can choose to use fresh sweet potatoes instead of frozen potatoes. Take one or two sweet potatoes, peel them, and cut them into 1-inch-thick strips with a sharp knife or mandolin. Use according to the recipe instructions. but you will need to increase the time for cooking.

Nutrition

Calories 323|Fat 10g|Saturated Fat 4g|Cholesterol 13mg|Sodium 138mg|Carbohydrates 58g|Fiber 7g|Protein 3g

184. Spicy Kale Chips with Yogurt Sauce

P Prep Time 10 m | P Cooking Time 5 m | 4 Servings

Ingredients

- 1 cup Greek yogurt
- 3 tablespoons lemon juice
- 2 tablespoons honey mustard
- ½ teaspoon dried oregano
- 1 bunch curly kale
- 2 tablespoons olive oil
- ½ teaspoon salt
- ⅛ teaspoon pepper

Directions

1. In a bowl, add together the yogurt, lemon juice, honey mustard, and oregano and set aside.
2. Remove the stems and ribs from the cabbage with a sharp knife. Cut the leaves into 2 to 3-inch pieces.
3. Toss the cabbage with olive oil, salt, and pepper. Massage the oil with your hands.
4. Fry the kale in batches until crisp, about 5 minutes, shaking the basket once during cooking. Serve with yogurt sauce.
Ingredient Tip: Kale is available in different varieties. Tuscan (also known as dinosaur or lacinato) is the most powerful and makes excellent marks. Kale, the variety widely found in grocery stores, can be slightly frozen when cooked in the deep fryer, but it's still delicious.

Nutrition

Calories 154|Fat 8g|Saturated Fat 2g|Cholesterol 3mg|Sodium 378mg|Carbohydrates 13g|Fiber 1g|Protein 8g

185. Phyllo Artichoke Triangles

P Prep Time 15 m | P Cooking Time 9 m | 18 Servings

Ingredients

- ¼ cup ricotta cheese
- 1 egg white
- ⅓ cup minced drained artichoke hearts
- 3 tablespoons grated mozzarella cheese
- ½ teaspoon dried thyme
- 6 sheets frozen phyllo dough, thawed
- 2 tablespoons melted butter

Directions

1. In a bowl, combine ricotta cheese, egg white, artichoke hearts, mozzarella cheese, and thyme and mix well.
2. Cover the dough with a damp kitchen towel while you work so it doesn't dry out. Using one sheet at a time, lay it out on your work surface and cut into thirds lengthwise.
3. Apply 1½ tsp of filling on each strip at the base. Fold the bottom-right edge of the sheet over the filling to meet the other side in a triangle, then continue folding into a triangle. Brush each angle with butter to seal the edges. Repeat with the remaining dough and filling.
4. Bake, 7 at a time, for about 3 to 4 minutes or until the sex is golden and crisp.
5. Replacement Tip: You can use anything in this filling in place of artichoke hearts. Try spinach, minced shrimp, cooked sausage or keep vegetarian and use all the grated cheese.

Nutrition

Calories 271|Fat 17g|Saturated Fat 7g|Cholesterol 19mg |Sodium 232mg|Carbohydrates 23g|Fiber 5g|Protein 9g

186. Arancini

P Prep Time 15 m | P Cooking Time 22 m | 16 Servings

Ingredients

- 2 eggs, beaten
- 1½ cups panko bread crumbs, divided
- ½ cup grated Parmesan cheese
- 2 tablespoons minced fresh basil
- 2 cups cooked rice or leftover risotto
- 16 ¾-inch cubes mozzarella cheese

- 2 tablespoons olive oil

Directions

1. In a medium bowl, add together the rice, eggs, a cup of breadcrumbs, Parmesan, and basil. Shape this mixture into 16 1-inch balls.
2. Create a hole in each of the balls with your finger and place a cube of mozzarella. Glue the rice mixture firmly around the cheese.
3. On a shallow plate, add together the remaining 1 cup of breadcrumbs with the olive oil and mix well. Wrap the rice balls in the breadcrumbs for color.
4. Cook the arancini in batches for 8 to 11 minutes or until golden brown.

Did you know that in Italy, arancini, also called frittata or rice soup, is sold on the street as a snack? They have grown much larger in this country, the size of an orange, and are often cone-shaped.

Nutrition

Calories 378 | Fat: 11g|Saturated Fat 4g|Cholesterol 57mg|Sodium 361mg|Carbohydrates 53g|Fiber 2g|Protein 16g

187. Pesto Bruschetta

P Prep Time 10 m | P Cooking Time 8 m | 4 Servings

Ingredients

- 8 slices French bread, ½ inch thick
- 2 tablespoons softened butter
- 1 cup shredded mozzarella cheese
- ½ cup basil pesto
- 1 cup chopped grape tomatoes
- 2 green onions, thinly sliced

Directions

1. Butter the bread and place the butter in the deep fryer basket. Bake 3 to 5 minutes or until bread is lightly golden.
2. Take the bread out of the basket and fill each piece with a little cheese. Return to the basket in batches and bake until cheese is melted, for about 1 to 3 minutes.
3. Meanwhile, combine pesto, tomatoes, and chives in a small bowl.
4. When the cheese is melted, remove the bread from the fryer and place it on a plate. Fill each slice with a little pesto mix and serve.

Nutrition

Calories: 462| Fat 25g|Saturated Fat 10g|Cholesterol 38mg|Sodium 822mg |Carbohydrates 41g|Fiber 3g|Protein 19g

188. Fried Tortellini with Spicy Dipping Sauce

P Prep Time 8 m | P Cooking Time 20 m | 4 Servings

Ingredients

- ¾ cup mayonnaise
- 2 tablespoons mustard
- 1 egg
- ½ cup flour
- ½ teaspoon dried oregano
- 1½ cups bread crumbs
- 2 tablespoons olive oil
- 2 cups frozen cheese tortellini

Directions

1.   In a small bowl, add together the mayonnaise and mustard and mix well. Set aside.
2.   In a shallow bowl, beat the egg. In a separate bowl, combine the flour and oregano. In another bowl, combine the breadcrumbs and olive oil and mix well.
3.   Add the tortellini, a few at a time, to the egg, then the flour, then the egg again, then the breadcrumbs to coat. Place in the fryer basket, cooking in batches.
4.   Air fry for about 10 minutes, stirring halfway through cooking time, or until tortellini are crisp and golden on the outside. Serve with mayonnaise.

Nutrition

Calories 698| Fat 31g|Saturated Fat 4g|Cholesterol 66mg|Sodium 832mg|Carbohydrates 88g|Fiber 3g|Protein 18g

189. Peanut Butter Banana Bread

P Prep Time 15 m | P Cooking Time 40 m | 6 Servings

Ingredients:

- 1 cup plus 1 tablespoon all-purpose flour
- ¼ teaspoon baking soda
- 1 teaspoon baking powder
- ¼ teaspoon salt
- 1 large egg
- 1/3 cup granulated sugar
- ¼ cup canola oil
- 2 tablespoons creamy peanut butter
- 2 tablespoons sour cream
- 1 teaspoon vanilla extract
- 2 medium ripe bananas, peeled and mashed
- ¾ cup walnuts, roughly chopped

Directions:

1.   In a bowl and mix the flour, baking powder, baking soda, and salt together.
2.   In another large bowl, add the egg, sugar, oil, peanut butter, sour cream, and vanilla extract and beat until well combined.
3.   Add the bananas and beat until well combined.
4.   Add the flour mixture and mix until just combined.
5.   Gently, fold in the walnuts.
6.   Place the mixture into a lightly greased pan.
7.   Press "Power Button" of Air Fry Oven and turn the dial to select the "Air Crisp" mode.
8.   Press the Time button and again turn the dial to set the cooking time to 40 minutes
9.   Now push the Temp button and rotate the dial to set the temperature at 330 degrees F.
10.   Press "Start/Pause" button to start.
11.   When the unit beeps to show that it is preheated, open the lid.
12.   Arrange the pan in "Air Fry Basket" and insert in the oven.
13.   Place the pan onto a wire rack to cool for about 10 minutes
14.   Carefully, invert the bread onto wire rack to cool completely before slicing.
15.   Cut the bread into desired-sized slices and serve.

Nutrition:

Calories 384 Fat 23 g Carbs 39.3 g Protein 8.9 g

190. Chocolate Banana Bread

P Prep Time 15 m | P Cooking Time 20 m | 8 Servings
Ingredients:
- 2 cups flour
- ½ teaspoon baking soda
- ½ teaspoon baking powder
- ½ teaspoon salt
- ¾ cup sugar
- 1/3 cup butter, softened
- 3 eggs
- 1 tablespoon vanilla extract
- 1 cup milk
- ½ cup bananas, peeled and mashed
- 1 cup chocolate chips

Directions:
1. In a bowl, mix together the flour, baking soda, baking powder, and salt.
2. In another large bowl, add the butter, and sugar and beat until light and fluffy.
3. Add the eggs, and vanilla extract and whisk until well combined.
4. Add the flour mixture and mix until well combined.
5. Add the milk, and mashed bananas and mix well.
6. Gently, fold in the chocolate chips. Place the mixture into a lightly greased loaf pan.
7. Press "Power Button" of Air Fry Oven and turn the dial to select the "Air Crisp" mode.
8. Press the Time button and again turn the dial to set the cooking time to 20 minutes
9. Now push the Temp button and rotate the dial to set the temperature at 360 degrees F.
10. Press "Start/Pause" button to start.When the unit beeps to show that it is preheated, open the lid.
11. Arrange the pan in "Air Fry Basket" and insert in the oven.
12. Place the pan onto a wire rack to cool for about 10 minutesCarefully, invert the bread onto wire rack to cool completely before slicing.
13. Cut the bread into desired-sized slices and serve.

Nutrition:
Calories 416 Fat 16.5 g Carbs 59.2 g Protein 8.1 g

191. Allspice Chicken Wings

P Prep Time 10 m | P Cooking Time 45 m | 8 Servings
Ingredients:
- ½ tsp celery salt
- ½ tsp bay leaf powder
- ½ tsp ground black pepper
- ½ tsp paprika
- ¼ tsp dry mustard
- ¼ tsp cayenne pepper
- ¼ tsp allspice
- 2 pounds chicken wings

Directions:
1. Grease the air fryer basket and preheat to 340 F. In a bowl, mix celery salt, bay leaf powder, black pepper, paprika, dry mustard, cayenne pepper, and allspice. Coat the wings thoroughly in this mixture.

2.	Arrange the wings in an even layer in the basket of the air fryer. Cook the chicken until it's no longer pink around the bone, for 30 minutes then, increase the temperature to 380 F and cook for 6 minutes more, until crispy on the outside.

Nutrition:
Calories 332 Fat 10.1 g Carbs 31.3 g Protein 12 g

192. Friday Night Pineapple Sticky Ribs

P Prep Time 10 m | P Cooking Time 20 m | 4 Servings

Ingredients:
- 2 lb. cut spareribs
- 7 oz salad dressing
- 1 (5-oz) can pineapple juice
- 2 cups water
- Garlic salt to taste
- Salt and black pepper

Directions:
1.	Sprinkle the ribs with salt and pepper, and place them in a saucepan. Pour water and cook the ribs for 12 minutes on high heat.
2.	Dry out the ribs and arrange them in the fryer; sprinkle with garlic salt. Cook it for 15minutes at 390 F.
3.	Prepare the sauce by combining the salad dressing and the pineapple juice. Serve the ribs drizzled with the sauce.

Nutrition:
Calories 316 Fat 3.1 g Carbs 1.9 g Protein 5 g

193. Egg Roll Wrapped With Cabbage And Prawns

P Prep Time 10 m | P Cooking Time 40 m | 4 Servings

Ingredients:
- 2 tbsp vegetable oil
- 1-inch piece fresh ginger, grated
- 1 tbsp minced garlic
- 1 carrot, cut into strips
- ¼ cup chicken broth
- 2 tbsp reduced-sodium soy sauce
- 1 tbsp sugar
- 1 cup shredded Napa cabbage
- 1 tbsp sesame oil
- 8 cooked prawns, minced
- 1 egg
- 8 egg roll wrappers

Directions:
1.	In a skillet over high heat, heat vegetable oil, and cook ginger and garlic for 40 seconds, until fragrant. Stir in carrot and cook for another 2 minutes Pour in chicken broth, soy sauce, and sugar and bring to a boil.
2.	Add cabbage and let simmer until softened, for 4 minutes Remove skillet from the heat and stir in sesame oil. Let cool for 15 minutes Strain cabbage mixture, and fold in minced prawns. Whisk an egg in a small bowl. Fill each egg roll wrapper with prawn mixture, arranging the mixture just below the center of the wrapper.

3.   Fold the bottom part over the filling and tuck under. Fold in both sides and tightly roll up. Use the whisked egg to seal the wrapper. Repeat until all egg rolls are ready. Place the rolls into a greased air fryer basket, spray them with oil and cook for 12 minutes at 370 F, turning once halfway through.
Nutrition:
Calories 215 Fat 7.9 g Carbs 6.7 g Protein 8 g

194. Sesame Garlic Chicken Wings

P Prep Time 10 m | P Cooking Time 40 m | 4 Servings
Ingredients:
- 1-pound chicken wings
- 1 cup soy sauce, divided
- ½ cup brown sugar
- ½ cup apple cider vinegar
- 2 tbsp fresh ginger, minced
- 2 tbsp fresh garlic, minced
- 1 tsp finely ground black pepper
- 2 tbsp cornstarch
- 2 tbsp cold water
- 1 tsp sesame seeds

Directions:
1.   In a bowl, add chicken wings, and pour in half cup soy sauce. Refrigerate for 20 minutes; Dry out and pat dry. Arrange the wings in the air fryer and cook for 30 minutes at 380 F, turning once halfway through. Make sure you check them towards the end to avoid overcooking.
2.   In a skillet and over medium heat, stir sugar, half cup soy sauce, vinegar, ginger, garlic, and black pepper. Cook until sauce has reduced slightly, about 4 to 6 minutes
3.   Dissolve 2 tbsp of cornstarch in cold water, in a bowl, and stir in the slurry into the sauce, until it thickens, for 2 minutes Pour the sauce over wings and sprinkle with sesame seeds.
Nutrition:
Calories 413 Fat 8.3 g Carbs 7 g Protein 8.3 g

195. Savory Chicken Nuggets With Parmesan Cheese

P Prep Time 5 m | P Cooking Time 20 m | 4 Servings
Ingredients:
- 1 lb. chicken breast, boneless, skinless, cubed
- ½ tsp ground black pepper
- ¼ tsp kosher salt
- ¼ tsp seasoned salt
- 2 tbsp olive oil
- 5 tbsp plain breadcrumbs
- 2 tbsp panko breadcrumbs
- 2 tbsp grated Parmesan cheese

Directions:
1.   Preheat the air fryer to 380 F and grease. Season the chicken with pepper, kosher salt, and seasoned salt; set aside. In a bowl, pour olive oil. In a separate bowl, add crumb, and Parmesan cheese.
2.   Place the chicken pieces in the oil to coat, then dip into breadcrumb mixture, and transfer to the air fryer. Work in batches if needed. Lightly spray chicken with cooking spray.

3.   Cook the chicken for 10 minutes, flipping once halfway through. Cook until golden brown on the outside and no more pink on the inside.
Nutrition:
Calories 312 Fat 8.9 g Carbs 7 g Protein 10 g

196. Butternut Squash With Thyme

P Prep Time 5 m | P Cooking Time 20 m | 4 Servings
Ingredients:
- 2 cups peeled, butternut squash, cubed
- 1 tbsp olive oil
- ¼ tsp salt
- ¼ tsp black pepper
- ¼ tsp dried thyme
- 1 tbsp finely chopped fresh parsley

Directions:
1.   In a bowl, add squash, oil, salt, pepper, and thyme, and toss until squash is well-coated.
2.   Place squash in the air fryer and cook for 14 minutes at 360 F.
3.   When ready, sprinkle with freshly chopped parsley and serve chilled.
Nutrition:
Calories 219 Fat 4.3 g Carbs 9.4 g Protein 7.8 g

197. Chicken Breasts In Golden Crumb

P Prep Time 10 m | P Cooking Time 25 m | 4 Servings
Ingredients:
- 1 ½ lb. chicken breasts, boneless, cut into strips
- 1 egg, lightly beaten
- 1 cup seasoned breadcrumbs
- Salt and black pepper to taste
- ½ tsp dried oregano

Directions:
1.   Preheat the air fryer to 390 F. Season the chicken with oregano, salt, and black pepper. In a small bowl, whisk in some salt and pepper to the beaten egg. In a separate bowl, add the crumbs. Dip chicken tenders in the egg wash, then in the crumbs.
2.   Roll the strips in the breadcrumbs and press firmly, so the breadcrumbs stick well. Spray the chicken tenders with cooking spray and arrange them in the air fryer. Cook for 14 minutes, until no longer pink in the center, and nice and crispy on the outside.
Nutrition:
Calories 223 Fat 3.2 g Carbs 4.3 g Protein 5 g

198. Yogurt Chicken Tacos

P Prep Time 5 m | P Cooking Time 20 m | 4 Servings
Ingredients:
- 1 cup cooked chicken, shredded
- 1 cup shredded mozzarella cheese
- ¼ cup salsa
- ¼ cup Greek yogurt
- Salt and ground black pepper
- 8 flour tortillas

Directions:

1.   In a bowl, mix chicken, cheese, salsa, and yogurt, and season with salt and pepper. Spray one side of the tortilla with cooking spray. Lay 2 tbsp of the chicken mixture at the center of the non-oiled side of each tortilla.

2.   Roll tightly around the mixture. Arrange taquitos into your air fryer basket, without overcrowding. Cook in batches if needed. Place the seam side down, or it will unravel during cooking crisps.

3.   Cook it for 12 to 14 minutes, or until crispy, at 380 F.

Nutrition:

Calories 312 Fat 3 g Carbs 6.5 g Protein 6.2 g

199. Flawless Kale Chips

P Prep Time 5 m | P Cooking Time 20 m | 4 Servings

Ingredients:

- 4 cups chopped kale leaves; stems removed
- 2 tbsp olive oil
- 1 tsp garlic powder
- ½ tsp salt
- ¼ tsp onion powder
- ¼ tsp black pepper

Directions:

1.   In a bowl, mix kale and oil together, until well-coated. Add in garlic, salt, onion, and pepper and toss until well-coated. Arrange half the kale leaves to air fryer, in a single layer.

2.   Cook for 8 minutes at 350 F, shaking once halfway through. Remove chips to a sheet to cool; do not touch.

Nutrition:

Calories 312 Fat 5.3 g Carbs 5 g Protein 7 g

200. Cheese Fish Balls

P Prep Time 5 m | P Cooking Time 40 m | 6 Servings

Ingredients:

- 1 cup smoked fish, flaked
- 2 cups cooked rice
- 2 eggs, lightly beaten
- 1 cup grated Grana Padano cheese
- ¼ cup finely chopped thyme
- Salt and black pepper to taste
- 1 cup panko crumbs

Directions:

1.   In a bowl, add fish, rice, eggs, Parmesan cheese, thyme, salt and pepper into a bowl; stir to combine. Shape the mixture into 12 even-sized balls. Roll the balls in the crumbs then spray with oil.

2.   Arrange the balls into the fryer and cook for 16 minutes at 400 F, until crispy.

Nutrition:

Calories 234 Fat 5.2 g Carbs 4.3 g Protein 6.2 g

DESSERT RECIPES

201. Angel Food Cake

P Prep Time 10 m | P Cooking Time 30 m | 12 Servings

Ingredients

- ¼ cup butter, melted
- 1 cup powdered erythritol
- 1 teaspoon strawberry extract
- 12 egg whites
- 2 teaspoons cream of tartar
- A pinch of salt

Directions

1. Preheat the air fryer for 5 minutes.
2. Mix the egg whites together with the cream of tartar.
3. Use a hand mixer and whisk until white and fluffy.
4. Add the rest of the ingredients except for the butter and whisk for another minute.
5. Pour into a baking dish.
6. Place in the oven basket and cook for 30 minutes at 4000F or if a toothpick inserted in the middle comes out clean.
7. Drizzle with melted butter once cooled.

Nutrition

Calories 65|Carbohydrates 1.8g|Protein 3.1g|Fat 5g

202. Apple Pie in Air Fryer

P Prep Time 15 m | P Cooking Time 35 m | 4 Servings

Ingredients

- ½ teaspoon vanilla extract
- 1 beaten egg
- 1 large apple, chopped
- 1 Pillsbury Refrigerator pie crust
- 1 tablespoon butter
- 1 tablespoon ground cinnamon
- 1 tablespoon raw sugar
- 2 tablespoon sugar
- 2 teaspoons lemon juice
- Baking spray

Directions

1. Lightly grease baking pan of the air fryer with cooking spray. Spread the pie crust on the rare part of the pan up to the sides.
2. In a bowl, make a mixture of vanilla, sugar, cinnamon, lemon juice, and apples. Pour on top of pie crust. Top apples with butter slices.
3. Cover apples with the other pie crust. Pierce with a knife the tops of the pie.
4. Spread whisked egg on top of crust and sprinkle sugar.
5. Cover with foil.
6. For 25 minutes, cook on 390oF.
7. Remove foil cook for 10 minutes at 330oF until tops are browned.
8. Serve and enjoy.

Nutrition

Calories 372|Carbs 44.7g|Protein 4.2g|Fat 19.6g

203. Apple-Toffee Upside-Down Cake

P Prep Time 10 m | P Cooking Time 30 m | 9 Servings

Ingredients

- ¼ cup almond butter
- ¼ cup sunflower oil
- ½ cup walnuts, chopped
- ¾ cup + 3 tablespoon coconut sugar
- ¾ cup water
- 1 ½ teaspoon mixed spice
- 1 cup plain flour
- 1 lemon, zest
- 1 teaspoon baking soda
- 1 teaspoon vinegar
- 3 baking apples, cored and sliced

Directions

1. Preheat the air fryer to 3900F.
2. In a skillet, melt the almond butter and 3 tablespoons sugar. Pour the mixture over a baking dish that will fit in the air fryer. Arrange the slices of apples on top. Set aside.
3. In a mixing bowl, combine flour, ¾ cup sugar, and baking soda. Add the mixed spice.
4. In a different bowl, mix the water, oil, vinegar, and lemon zest. Stir in the chopped walnuts.
5. Combine the wet ingredients to the dry ingredients until well combined.
6. Pour over the tin with apple slices.
7. Bake for 30 minutes or until a toothpick inserted comes out clean.

Nutrition

Calories 335|Carbohydrates 39.6g|Protein 3.8g|Fat 17.9g

204. Banana-Choco Brownies

P Prep Time 15 m | P Cooking Time 30 m | 12 Servings

Ingredients

- 2 cups almond flour
- 2 teaspoons baking powder
- ½ teaspoon baking powder
- ½ teaspoon baking soda
- ½ teaspoon salt
- 1 over-ripe banana
- 3 large eggs
- ½ teaspoon stevia powder
- ¼ cup coconut oil
- 1 tablespoon vinegar
- 1/3 cup almond flour
- 1/3 cup cocoa powder

Directions

1. Preheat the air fryer for 5 minutes.
2. Add together all ingredients in a food processor and pulse until well combined.
3. Pour into a skillet that will fit in the deep fryer.

4. Place in the fryer basket and cook for 30 minutes at 3500F or if a toothpick inserted in the middle comes out clean.

Nutrition

Calories 75|Carbohydrates 2.1g |Protein 1.7g|Fat 6.6g

205. Blueberry & Lemon Cake

P Prep Time 10 m | P Cooking Time 17 m | 4 Servings

Ingredients

- 2 eggs
- 1 cup blueberries
- zest from 1 lemon
- juice from 1 lemon
- 1 tsp. vanilla
- brown sugar for topping (a little sprinkling on top of each muffin-less than a teaspoon)
- 2 1/2 cups self-rising flour
- 1/2 cup Monk Fruit (or use your preferred sugar)
- 1/2 cup cream
- 1/4 cup avocado oil (any light cooking oil)

Directions

1. In mixing bowl, beat well the wet ingredients. Stir in dry ingredients and mix thoroughly.
2. Lightly grease baking pan of the air fryer with cooking spray. Pour in batter.
3. For 12 minutes, cook on 330F.
4. Let it stand in the air fryer for 5 minutes.
5. Serve and enjoy.

Nutrition

Calories 589|Carbs 76.7g|Protein 13.5g|Fat 25.3g

206. Bread Pudding with Cranberry

P Prep Time 20 m | P Cooking Time 45 m | 4 Servings

Ingredients

- 1-1/2 cups milk
- 2-1/2 eggs
- 1/2 cup cranberries1 teaspoon butter
- 1/4 cup golden raisins
- 1/8 teaspoon ground cinnamon
- 3/4 cup heavy whipping cream
- 3/4 teaspoon lemon zest
- 3/4 teaspoon kosher salt
- 2 tbsp. and 1/4 cup white sugar
- 3/4 French baguettes, cut into 2-inch slices
- 3/8 vanilla bean, split and seeds scraped away

Directions

1. Lightly grease baking pan of the air fryer with cooking spray. Spread baguette slices, cranberries, and raisins.
2. In a blender, blend well vanilla bean, cinnamon, salt, lemon zest, eggs, sugar, and cream. Pour over baguette slices. Let it soak for an hour.
3. Cover pan with foil.
4. For 35 minutes, cook on 330F.

113

5. Let it rest for 10 minutes.
6. Serve and enjoy.

Nutrition

Calories 581 |Carbs 76.1g|Protein 15.8g|Fat 23.7g

207. Cherries 'n Almond Flour Bars

P Prep Time 15 m | P Cooking Time 35 m | 12 Servings

Ingredients

- ¼ cup of water
- ½ cup butter softened
- ½ teaspoon salt
- ½ teaspoon vanilla
- 1 ½ cups almond flour
- 1 cup erythritol
- 1 cup fresh cherries, pitted
- 1 tablespoon xanthan gum
- 2 eggs

Directions

1. In a medium bowl, make a mixture of the first 6 ingredients to form a dough.
2. Press the batter onto a baking sheet that will fit in the air fryer.
3. Place in the fryer and bake for 10 minutes at 375F.
4. Meanwhile, mix the cherries, water, and xanthan gum in a bowl.
5. Scoop out the dough and pour over the cherry.
6. Return to the fryer and cook for another 25 minutes at 3750F.

Nutrition

Calories 99 |Carbohydrates 2.1g |Protein 1.8g|Fat 9.3g

208. Cherry-Choco Bars

P Prep Time 5 m | P Cooking Time 15 m | 8 Servings

Ingredients

- ¼ teaspoon salt
- ½ cup almonds, sliced
- ½ cup chia seeds
- ½ cup dark chocolate, chopped
- ½ cup dried cherries, chopped
- ½ cup prunes, pureed
- ½ cup quinoa, cooked
- ¾ cup almond butter
- 1/3 cup honey
- 2 cups old-fashioned oats
- 2 tablespoon coconut oil

Directions

1. Preheat the air fryer to 3750F.
2. In a bowl, combine the oats, quinoa, chia seeds, almond, cherries, and chocolate.
3. In a saucepan, heat the almond butter, honey, and coconut oil.
4. Pour the butter mixture over the dry mixture. Add salt and prunes.
5. Mix until well combined.
6. Pour over a baking dish that can fit inside the air fryer.

7. Cook for 15 minutes.
8. Allow settling for an hour before slicing into bars.

Nutrition
Calories 321|Carbohydrates 35g|Protein 7g|Fat 17g

209. Chocolate Chip in a Mug

P Prep Time 10 m | P Cooking Time 20 m | 6 Servings

Ingredients
- ¼ cup walnuts, shelled and chopped
- ½ cup butter, unsalted
- ½ cup dark chocolate chips
- ½ cup erythritol
- ½ teaspoon baking soda
- ½ teaspoon salt
- 1 tablespoon vanilla extract
- 2 ½ cups almond flour
- 2 large eggs, beaten

Directions
1. Preheat the air fryer for 5 minutes.
2. Combine all ingredients in a mixing bowl.
3. Place in greased mugs.
4. Bake in the air fryer oven for 20 minutes at 3750F.

Nutrition
Calories 234|Carbohydrates 4.9g|Protein 2.3g|Fat 22.8g

210. Choco-Peanut Mug Cake

P Prep Time 10 m | P Cooking Time 20 m | 6 Servings

Ingredients
- ¼ teaspoon baking powder
- ½ teaspoon vanilla extract
- 1 egg
- 1 tablespoon heavy cream
- 1 tablespoon peanut butter
- 1 teaspoon butter, softened
- 2 tablespoon erythritol
- 2 tablespoons cocoa powder, unsweetened

Directions
1. Preheat the air fryer for 5 minutes.
2. Combine all ingredients in a mixing bowl.
3. Pour into a greased mug.
4. Place in the air fryer oven basket and cook for 20 minutes at 4000F or if a toothpick inserted in the middle comes out clean.

Nutrition
Calories 293 |Carbohydrates 8.5g|Protein 12.4g|Fat 23.3g

211. Coco-Lime Bars

P Prep Time 10 m | P Cooking Time 20 m | 3 Servings

Ingredients

- ¼ cup almond flour
- ¼ cup coconut oil
- ¼ cup dried coconut flakes
- ¼ teaspoon salt
- ½ cup lime juice
- ¾ cup coconut flour
- 1 ¼ cup erythritol powder
- 1 tablespoon lime zest
- 4 eggs

Directions
1. Preheat the air fryer for 5 minutes.
2. Combine all ingredients in a mixing bowl.
3. Place in the greased mug.
4. Bake in the air fryer oven for 20 minutes at 375F.

Nutrition
Calories 506 |Carbohydrates 21.9g|Protein 19.3g|Fat 37.9g

212. Coconut 'n Almond Fat Bombs

P Prep Time 5 m | P Cooking Time 15 m | 12 Servings
Ingredients
- ¼ cup almond flour
- ½ cup shredded coconut
- 1 tablespoon coconut oil
- 1 tablespoon vanilla extract
- 2 tablespoons liquid stevia
- 3 egg whites

Directions
1. Preheat the air fryer for 5 minutes.
2. Combine all ingredients in a mixing bowl.
3. Form small balls using your hands.
4. Place in the air fryer oven basket and cook for 15 minutes at 4000F.

Nutrition
Calories 23 |Carbohydrates 0.7g|Protein 1.1g|Fat 1.8g

213. Coconutty Lemon Bars

P Prep Time 10 m | P Cooking Time 25 m | 12 Servings
Ingredients
- ¼ cup cashew
- ¼ cup fresh lemon juice, freshly squeezed
- ¾ cup coconut milk
- ¾ cup erythritol
- 1 cup desiccated coconut
- 1 teaspoon baking powder
- 2 eggs, beaten
- 2 tablespoons coconut oil
- A dash of salt

Directions
1. Preheat the air fryer for 5 minutes.

2.   In a mixing bowl, combine all ingredients.
3.   Use a hand mixer to mix everything.
4.   Pour into a baking bowl that will fit in the air fryer.
5.   Bake for 25 minutes at 350F or until a toothpick inserted in the middle comes out clean.

Nutrition

Calories 118|Carbohydrates 3.9g|Protein 2.6g |Fat 10.2g

214. Coffee 'n Blueberry Cake

P Prep Time 15 m | P Cooking Time 35 m | 6 Servings

Ingredients

- 1 cup white sugar
- 1 egg
- 1/2 cup butter, softened
- 1/2 cup fresh or frozen blueberries
- 1/2 cup sour cream
- 1/2 teaspoon baking powder
- 1/2 teaspoon ground cinnamon
- 1/2 teaspoon vanilla extract
- 1/4 cup brown sugar
- 1/4 cup chopped pecans
- 1/8 teaspoon salt
- 1-1/2 teaspoons confectioners' sugar for dusting
- 3/4 cup and 1 tablespoon all-purpose flour

Directions

1.   In a small bowl, whisk well pecans, cinnamon, and brown sugar.
2.   In a blender, blend well all wet ingredients. Add dry ingredients except for confectioner's sugar and blueberries. Blend well until smooth and creamy.
3.   Lightly grease baking pan of the air fryer with cooking spray.
4.   Pour half of the batter in pan. Sprinkle a little of the pecan mixture on top. Pour the remaining batter and then top with the remaining pecan mixture.
5.   Cover pan with foil.
6.   For 35 minutes, cook on 330oF.
7.   Serve and enjoy with a dusting of confectioner's sugar.

Nutrition

Calories 471|Carbs 59.5g|Protein 4.1g |Fat 24.0g

215. Date & Walnut Bread

P Prep Time 15 m | P Cooking Time 35 m | 5 Servings

Ingredients:

- 1 cup dates, pitted and sliced
- ¾ cup walnuts, chopped
- 1 tablespoon instant coffee powder
- 1 tablespoon hot water
- 1¼ cups plain flour
- ¼ teaspoon salt
- ½ teaspoon baking powder
- ½ teaspoon baking soda
- ½ cup condensed milk

- ½ cup butter, softened
- ½ teaspoon vanilla essence

Directions:

1 In a large bowl, add the dates, butter and top with the hot water.
2 Set aside for about 30 minutes
3 Dry out well and set aside.
4 In a small bowl, add the coffee powder and hot water and mix well.
5 In a large bowl, mix together the flour, baking powder, baking soda and salt.
6 In another large bowl, add the condensed milk and butter and beat until smooth.
7 Add the flour mixture, coffee mixture and vanilla essence and mix until well combined.
8 Fold in dates and ½ cup of walnut.
9 Line a baking pan with a lightly greased parchment paper.
10 Place the mixture into the prepared pan and sprinkle with the remaining walnuts.
11 Press "Power Button" of Air Fry Oven and turn the dial to select the "Air Crisp" mode.
12 Press the Time button and again turn the dial to set the cooking time to 35 minutes
13 Now push the Temp button and rotate the dial to set the temperature at 320 degrees F.
14 Press "Start/Pause" button to start.
15 When the unit beeps to show that it is preheated, open the lid.
16 Arrange the pan in "Air Fry Basket" and insert in the oven.
17 Place the pan onto a wire rack to cool for about 10 minutes
18 Carefully, invert the bread onto wire rack to cool completely before slicing.
19 Cut the bread into desired-sized slices and serve.

Nutrition:

Calories 593 |Fat 32.6 g |Carbs 69.4 g | Protein 11.2 g

216. Brown Sugar Banana Bread

P Prep Time 15 m | P Cooking Time 30 m | 4 Servings

Ingredients:

- 1 egg
- 1 ripe banana, peeled and mashed
- ¼ cup milk
- tablespoons canola oil
- tablespoons brown sugar
- ¾ cup plain flour
- ½ teaspoon baking soda

Directions:

1 Line a very small baking pan with a greased parchment paper.
2 In a small bowl, add the egg and banana and beat well.
3 Add the milk, oil and sugar and beat until well combined.
4 Add the flour and baking soda and mix until just combined.
5 Place the mixture into prepared pan.
6 Press "Power Button" of Air Fry Oven and turn the dial to select the "Air Crisp" mode.
7 Press the Time button and again turn the dial to set the cooking time to 30 minutes
8 Now push the Temp button and rotate the dial to set the temperature at 320 degrees F.
9 Press "Start/Pause" button to start.
10 When the unit beeps to show that it is preheated, open the lid.
11 Arrange the pan in "Air Fry Basket" and insert in the oven.
12 Place the pan onto a wire rack to cool for about 10 minutes

13 Carefully, invert the bread onto wire rack to cool completely before slicing.
14 Cut the bread into desired-sized slices and serve.
Nutrition:
Calories 214 |Fat 8.7 g |Carbs 29.9 g |Protein 4.6 g

217. Cinnamon Banana Bread

P Prep Time 15 m | P Cooking Time 20 m | 8 Servings
Ingredients:
- 1 1/3 cups flour
- 2/3 cup sugar
- 1 teaspoon baking soda
- 1 teaspoon baking powder
- 1 teaspoon ground cinnamon
- 1 teaspoon salt
- ½ cup milk
- ½ cup olive oil
- bananas, peeled and sliced

Directions:
1 In the bowl of a stand mixer, add all the ingredients and mix well.
2 Grease a loaf pan.
3 Place the mixture into the prepared pan.
4 Press "Power Button" of Air Fry Oven and turn the dial to select the "Air Crisp" mode.
5 Press the Time button and again turn the dial to set the cooking time to 20 minutes
6 Now push the Temp button and rotate the dial to set the temperature at 330 degrees F.
7 Press "Start/Pause" button to start.
8 When the unit beeps to show that it is preheated, open the lid.
9 Arrange the pan in "Air Fry Basket" and insert in the oven.
10 Place the pan onto a wire rack to cool for about 10 minutes
11 Carefully, invert the bread onto wire rack to cool completely before slicing.
12 Cut the bread into desired-sized slices and serve.
Nutrition:
Calories 295| Fat 13.3g| Carbs 44 g | Protein 3.1 g

218.Banana & Walnut Bread

P Prep Time 15 m | P Cooking Time 25 m | 10 Servings
Ingredients:
- 1½ cups self-rising flour
- ¼ teaspoon bicarbonate of soda
- tablespoons plus 1 teaspoon butter
- 2/3 cup plus ½ tablespoon caster sugar
- medium eggs
- 3½ oz. walnuts, chopped
- cups bananas, peeled and mashed

Directions:
1 In a bowl, mix together the flour and bicarbonate of soda.
2 In another bowl, add the butter, and sugar and beat until pale and fluffy.
3 Add the eggs, one at a time along with a little flour and mix well.
4 Stir in the remaining flour and walnuts.

5 Add the bananas and mix until well combined.

6 Grease a loaf pan.

7 Place the mixture into the prepared pan.

8 Press "Power Button" of Air Fry Oven and turn the dial to select the "Air Crisp" mode.

9 Press the Time button and again turn the dial to set the cooking time to 10 minutes

10 Now push the Temp button and rotate the dial to set the temperature at 355 degrees F.

11 Press "Start/Pause" button to start.

12 When the unit beeps to show that it is preheated, open the lid.

13 Arrange the pan in "Air Fry Basket" and insert in the oven.

14 After 10 minutes of cooking, set the temperature at 338 degrees F for 15 minutes

15 Place the pan onto a wire rack to cool for about 10 minutes

16 Carefully, invert the bread onto wire rack to cool completely before slicing.

17 Cut the bread into desired-sized slices and serve.

Nutrition:

Calories 270 |Fat 12.8 g |Carbs 35.5 g |Protein 5.8 g

219. Banana & Raisin Bread

P Prep Time 15 m | P Cooking Time 40 m | 6 Servings

Ingredients:

- 1½ cups cake flour
- 1 teaspoon baking soda
- ½ teaspoon ground cinnamon
- Salt, to taste
- ½ cup vegetable oil
- eggs
- ½ cup sugar
- ½ teaspoon vanilla extract
- medium bananas, peeled and mashed
- ½ cup raisins, chopped finely

Directions:

1 In a large bowl, mix together the flour, baking soda, cinnamon, and salt.

2 In another bowl, beat well eggs and oil.

3 Add the sugar, vanilla extract, and bananas and beat until well combined.

4 Add the flour mixture and stir until just combined.

5 Place the mixture into a lightly greased baking pan and sprinkle with raisins.

6 With a piece of foil, cover the pan loosely.

7 Press "Power Button" of Air Fry Oven and turn the dial to select the "Air Bake" mode.

8 Press the Time button and again turn the dial to set the cooking time to 30 minutes

9 Now push the Temp button and rotate the dial to set the temperature at 300 degrees F.

10 Press "Start/Pause" button to start.

11 When the unit beeps to show that it is preheated, open the lid.

12 Arrange the pan in "Air Fry Basket" and insert in the oven.

13 After 30 minutes of cooking, set the temperature to 285 degrees F for 10 minutes

14 Place the pan onto a wire rack to cool for about 10 minutes

15 Carefully, invert the bread onto wire rack to cool completely before slicing.

16 Cut the bread into desired-sized slices and serve.

Nutrition:

Calories 448 |Fat 20.2 g| Carbs 63.9 g | Protein 6.1 g

220. 3-Ingredients Banana Bread

P Prep Time 10 m | P Cooking Time 20 m | 6 Servings

Ingredients:
- (6.4-oz.) banana muffin mix
- 1 cup water
- 1 ripe banana, peeled and mashed

Directions:
1 In a bowl, add all the ingredients and with a whisk, mix until well combined.
2 Place the mixture into a lightly greased loaf pan.
3 Press "Power Button" of Air Fry Oven and turn the dial to select the "Air Bake" mode.
4 Press the Time button and again turn the dial to set the cooking time to 20 minutes
5 Now push the Temp button and rotate the dial to set the temperature at 360 degrees F.
6 Press "Start/Pause" button to start.
7 When the unit beeps to show that it is preheated, open the lid.
8 Arrange the pan in "Air Fry Basket" and insert in the oven.
9 Place the pan onto a wire rack to cool for about 10 minutes
10 Carefully, invert the bread onto wire rack to cool completely before slicing.
11 Cut the bread into desired-sized slices and serve.

Nutrition:
Calories 144 |Fat 3.8 g| Carbs 25.5 g| Protein 1.9 g

221. Yogurt Banana Bread

P Prep Time 15 m | P Cooking Time 28 m | 5 Servings

Ingredients:
- 1 medium very ripe banana, peeled and mashed
- 1 large egg
- 1 tablespoon canola oil
- 1 tablespoon plain Greek yogurt
- ¼ teaspoon pure vanilla extract
- ½ cup all-purpose flour
- ¼ cup granulated white sugar
- ¼ teaspoon ground cinnamon
- ¼ teaspoon baking soda
- 1/8 teaspoon sea salt

Directions:
1 In a bowl, add the mashed banana, egg, oil, yogurt and vanilla and beat until well combined.
2 Add the flour, sugar, baking soda, cinnamon and salt and mix until just combined.
3 Place the mixture into a lightly greased mini loaf pan.
4 Press "Power Button" of Air Fry Oven and turn the dial to select the "Air Bake" mode.
5 Press the Time button and again turn the dial to set the cooking time to 28 minutes
6 Now push the Temp button and rotate the dial to set the temperature at 350 degrees F.
7 Press "Start/Pause" button to start.
8 When the unit beeps to show that it is preheated, open the lid.
9 Arrange the pan in "Air Fry Basket" and insert in the oven.
10 Place the pan onto a wire rack to cool for about 10 minutes
11 Carefully, invert the bread onto wire rack to cool completely before slicing.
12 Cut the bread into desired-sized slices and serve.

Nutrition:

Calories 145 |Fat 4 g| Carbs 25 g | Protein 3 g

222. Sour Cream Banana Bread

P Prep Time 15 m | P Cooking Time 37 m | 8 Servings

Ingredients:
- ¾ cup all-purpose flour
- ¼ teaspoon baking soda
- ¼ teaspoon salt
- ripe bananas, peeled and mashed
- ½ cup granulated sugar
- ¼ cup sour cream
- ¼ cup vegetable oil
- 1 large egg
- ½ teaspoon pure vanilla extract

Directions:
1 In a large bowl, mix together the flour, baking soda and salt.
2 In another bowl, add the bananas, egg, sugar, sour cream, oil and vanilla and beat until well combined.
3 Add the flour mixture and mix until just combined.
4 Place the mixture into a lightly greased pan. Press "Power Button" of Air Fry Oven and turn the dial to select the "Air Crisp" mode.
5 Press the Time button and again turn the dial to set the cooking time to 37 minutes
6 Now push the Temp button and rotate the dial to set the temperature at 310 degrees F. Press "Start/Pause" button to start.
7 When the unit beeps to show that it is preheated, open the lid. Arrange the pan in "Air Fry Basket" and insert in the oven.
8 Place the pan onto a wire rack to cool for about 10 minutes
9 Carefully, invert the bread onto wire rack to cool completely before slicing.
10 Cut the bread into desired-sized slices and serve.

Nutrition:
Calories 201| Fat 9.2g| Carbs 28.6g | Protein 2.6g

223. Peanut Butter Banana Bread

P Prep Time 15 m | P Cooking Time 40 m | 6 Servings

Ingredients:
- 1 cup plus 1 tablespoon all-purpose flour
- ¼ teaspoon baking soda
- 1 teaspoon baking powder
- ¼ teaspoon salt
- 1 large egg
- 1/3 cup granulated sugar
- ¼ cup canola oil
- tablespoons creamy peanut butter
- tablespoons sour cream
- 1 teaspoon vanilla extract
- medium ripe bananas, peeled and mashed
- ¾ cup walnuts, roughly chopped

Directions:

1 In a bowl and mix the flour, baking powder, baking soda, and salt together.
2 In another large bowl, add the egg, sugar, oil, peanut butter, sour cream, and vanilla extract and beat until well combined.
3 Add the bananas and beat until well combined.
4 Add the flour mixture and mix until just combined.
5 Gently, fold in the walnuts.
6 Place the mixture into a lightly greased pan.
7 Press "Power Button" of Air Fry Oven and turn the dial to select the "Air Crisp" mode.
8 Press the Time button and again turn the dial to set the cooking time to 40 minutes
9 Now push the Temp button and rotate the dial to set the temperature at 330 degrees F.
10 Press "Start/Pause" button to start.
11 When the unit beeps to show that it is preheated, open the lid.
12 Arrange the pan in "Air Fry Basket" and insert in the oven.
13 Place the pan onto a wire rack to cool for about 10 minutes
14 Carefully, invert the bread onto wire rack to cool completely before slicing.
15 Cut the bread into desired-sized slices and serve.
Nutrition:
Calories 384| Fat 23 g| Carbs 39.3 g | Protein 8.9 g

224. Cinnamon & Honey Apples With Hazelnuts

P Prep Time 13 m | P Cooking Time 10 m | 2 Servings
Ingredients
- 4 Apples
- 1 oz butter
- 1 oz breadcrumbs
- Zest of 1 orange
- 1 tbsp chopped hazelnuts
- 1 oz mixed seeds
- 1 tsp cinnamon
- 1 tbsp honey

Directions
1 Preheat air fryer on bake function to 350 f and core the apples. Make sure also to score their skin to prevent from splitting. Combine the remaining ingredients in a bowl; stuff the apples with the mixture and cook for 10 minutes. Serve topped with chopped hazelnuts.
Nutrition:
Calories: 1174, Protein: 22.74g, Fat: 82.57g, Carbs: 106.11g

225. Pan-Fried Bananas

P Prep Time 15 m | P Cooking Time 8-12 m | 8 Servings
Ingredients
- 2 bananas
- 1 tbsp vegetable oil
- 1 tbsp corn flour
- 1 egg white
- ¾ cup breadcrumbs

Directions

Preheat air fryer on toast function to 350 f. Combine oil and breadcrumbs in a bowl. Coat the bananas with the corn flour, brush with egg white, and dip in the breadcrumb mixture. Arrange on a lined baking sheet and cook for 8-12 minutes.

Nutrition:
Calories: 162, Protein: 1.93g, Fat: 5.6g, Carbs: 29.09g

226. Delicious Banana Pastry With Berries

P Prep Time 15 m | P Cooking Time 10-12 m | 2 Servings

Ingredients
- 2 bananas, sliced
- 1 tbsp honey
- 1 puff pastry sheets, cut into thin strips
- Fresh berries to serve

Directions
1 Preheat air fryer on airfry function to 340 f and place the banana slices into the cooking basket. Cover with the pastry strips and top with honey. Cook for 10-12 minutes on bake function. Serve with fresh berries.

Nutrition:
Calories: 253, Protein: 2.02g, Fat: 0.58g, Carbs: 66.38g

227. Easy Mocha Cake

P Prep Time 30 m | P Cooking Time 15 m | 2 Servings

Ingredients
- ¼ cup butter
- ½ tsp instant coffee
- tbsp black coffee, brewed
- 1 egg
- ¼ cup sugar
- ¼ cup flour
- 1 tsp cocoa powder
- A pinch of salt
- Powdered sugar, for icing

Directions
1. Preheat air fryer on bake function to 330 f and grease a small ring cake pan. Beat the sugar and egg together in a bowl. Beat in cocoa, instant and black coffees; stir in salt and flour. Transfer the batter to the prepared pan. Cook for 15 minutes. Dust with powdered sugar and serve.

Nutrition:
Calories: 377, Protein: 6.54g, Fat: 28.13g, Carbs: 25.65g

228. Choco Lava Cakes

P Prep Time 20 m | P Cooking Time 10 m | 4 Servings

Ingredients
- ½ oz butter, melted
- ½ tbsp sugar
- ½ tbsp self-rising flour
- ½ oz dark chocolate, melted
- 2 eggs

Directions

1.   Grease 4 ramekins with butter. Preheat air fryer on bake function to 375 f. Beat eggs and sugar until frothy. Stir in butter and chocolate; gently fold in the flour.
2.   Divide the mixture between the ramekins and bake in the fryer for 10 minutes. Let cool for 2 minutes before turning the cakes upside down onto serving plates.

Nutrition:
Calories: 428, Protein: 6.92g, Fat: 35.54g, Carbs: 21.06g

229. Mouthwatering Chocolate Soufflé

P Prep Time 25 m | P Cooking Time 14-18 m | 2 Servings

Ingredients

- 2 eggs, whites and yolks separated
- ¼ cup butter, melted
- 1 tbsp flour
- 1 tbsp sugar
- 1 oz chocolate, melted
- ½ tsp vanilla extract

Directions

1 Beat the yolks along with the sugar and vanilla extract; stir in butter, chocolate, and flour. Preheat air fryer on bake function to 330 f and whisk the whites until a stiff peak forms. Working in batches, gently combine the egg whites with the chocolate mixture. Divide the batter between two greased ramekins. Cook for 14-18 minutes.

Nutrition:
Calories: 455, Protein: 4.64g, Fat: 28.1g, Carbs: 46.38g

230. Maple Pecan Pie

P Prep Time 1 h 10 m | P Cooking Time 30 m | 4 Servings

Ingredients

- ¾ cup maple syrup
- 2 eggs
- ½ tsp salt
- ¼ tsp nutmeg
- ½ tsp cinnamon
- 1 tbsp almond butter
- 1 tbsp brown sugar
- ½ cup chopped pecans
- tbsp butter, melted
- 1 8-inch pie dough
- ¾ tsp vanilla extract

Directions

1.   Preheat air fryer on toast function to 350 f, and coat the pecans with the melted butter. Place the pecans in the fryer and toast them for 5 minutes. Place the pie crust into the baking pan, and scatter the pecans over.
2.   Whisk together all remaining ingredients in a bowl. Pour the maple mixture over the pecans. Set air fryer to 320 f and cook the pie for 25 minutes on bake function.

Nutrition:
Calories: 2403, Protein: 19.26g, Fat: 136.07g, Carbs: 278g

231. Tangerine Cake

P Prep Time 30 m | P Cooking Time 20 m | 8 Servings

Ingredients

- ¾ cup sugar
- cups flour
- ¼ cup olive oil
- ½ cup milk
- 1 tbsp. Cider vinegar
- ½ tbsp. Vanilla extract
- Juice and zest from 2 lemons
- Juice and zest from 1 tangerine
- Tangerine segments

Directions:

1. Mix in flour with sugar and turn.
2. Mix oil with vinegar, milk, vanilla extract, tangerine zest and lemon juice, then beat properly.
3. Put flour, turn properly, get mix into a cake pan, get in air fryer and cook at 360°f for 20 minutes.
4. Serve with tangerine segments over.

Nutrition:

Calories: 225, Protein: 3.75g, Fat: 7.58g, Carbs: 34.88g

232. Blueberry Pudding

P Prep Time 35 m | P Cooking Time 25 m | 6 Servings

Ingredients

- 1 cups flour
- 1 cups rolled oats
- 1 cups blueberries
- stick butter
- 1 cup walnuts
- tbsp. Maple syrup
- tbsp. Rosemary

Directions:

1. Spray blueberries smeared baking pan and keep.
2. Mix rolled oats with walnuts, flour, butter, rosemary and maple syrup, beat properly, put mix over blueberries, put all in air fryer and cook at 350° for 25 minutes.
3. Allow to cool, slice.
4. Serve.

Nutrition:

Calories: 778, Protein: 14.16g, Fat: 27.75g, Carbs: 136.5g

233. Cocoa And Almond Bars

P Prep Time 34 m | P Cooking Time 4 m | 6 Servings

Ingredients

- ¼ cup cocoa nibs
- 1 cup almonds
- 1 tbsp. Cocoa powder
- ¼ cup hemp seeds

- ¼ cup goji berries
- ¼ cup coconut
- 6 dates

Directions:

1 Blend almonds in food processor, put hemp seeds, cocoa powder, cocoa nibs, coconut, goji and beat properly.

2 Put dates, beat properly, spray on a lined baking sheet, get in air fryer and cook at 320°f for 4 minutes.

3 Slice into equal segment and allow in fridge for 30 minutes.

4 Serve.

Nutrition:

Calories: 76, Protein: 2.53g, Fat: 3.86g, Carbs: 11.82g

234. Chocolate And Pomegranate Bars

P Prep Time 2h 10 m | P Cooking Time 10 m | 6 Servings

Ingredients

- ½ cup milk
- 1 tbsp. Vanilla extract
- 1 and ½ cups dark chocolate
- ½ cup almonds
- ½ cup pomegranate seeds

Directions:

1.   Warm pan with milk over medium heat, put chocolate, turn for 5 minutes, remove heat, put half of the pomegranate seeds, vanilla extract and half of the nuts and turn.

2.   Put mix into a lined baking pan, spray, spread a pinch of salt, nuts, and remaining pomegranate, get in air fryer and cook at 300° f for 4 minutes.

3.   Allow in fridge for 2 hours then serve.

Nutrition:

Calories: 139, Protein: 2.37g, Fat: 8.17g, Carbs: 13.39g

235. Tomato Cake

P Prep Time 40 m | P Cooking Time 30 m | 4 Servings

Ingredients

- ½ cups flour
- 1 tbsp. Cinnamon powder
- 1 tbsp. Baking powder
- 1 tbsp. Baking soda
- ¾ cup maple syrup
- 1 cup tomatoes
- ½ cup olive oil
- tbsp. Apple cider vinegar

Directions:

1.   Mix in flour with baking soda, baking powder, maple syrup and cinnamon in a bowl then turn properly.

2.   Mix in tomatoes with vinegar and olive oil in another bowl and turn properly.

3.   Blend the 2 mixtures, turn properly, put into round pan, get into the fryer and cook at 360°f for 30 minutes.

4.   Allow to cool, divide.

5.   Serve.
Nutrition:
Calories: 519, Protein: 3.66g, Fat: 27.44g, Carbs: 66.54g

236. Berries Mix

P Prep Time 11 m | P Cooking Time 6 m | 4 Servings
Ingredients
- tbsp. Lemon juice
- ½ tbsp. Maple syrup
- 1 and ½ tbsp. Champagne vinegar
- 1 tbsp. Olive oil
- 1 lb. (453.592g) Strawberries
- 1 and ½ cups blueberries
- ¼ cup basil leaves

Directions:
1.   Mix in lemon juice with vinegar and maple syrup in a pan, boil over medium heat, put oil, strawberries and blueberries, turn, get in air fryer and cook at 310°f for 6 minutes.
2.   Dust basil over then serve.
Nutrition:
Calories: 138, Protein: 1.21g, Fat: 3.95g, Carbs: 26.74g

237. Passion Fruit Pudding

P Prep Time 50 m | P Cooking Time 40 m | 6 Servings
Ingredients
- cup paleo passion fruit curd
- passion fruits
- ½ oz. Maple syrup
- eggs
- oz. Ghee
- and ½ oz. Almond milk
- ½ cup almond flour
- ½ tbsp. Baking powder

Directions:
1 Mix in the half of the fruit curd with passion fruit seeds and pulp in a bowl, turn and slice into 6 heat proof ramekins.
2 Beat eggs with ghee, the rest of the curd, maple syrup, baking powder, flour and milk then turn properly.
3 Share mix into the ramekins also, get in the fryer and cook at 200° f for 40 minutes.
4 Allow pudding to cool.
5 Serve.
Nutrition:
Calories: 214, Protein: 6.33g, Fat: 9.92g, Carbs: 26.95g

238. Air Fried Apples

P Prep Time 27 m | P Cooking Time 17 m | 4 Servings
Ingredients
- 4 big apples
- A handful raisins

- 1 tbsp. Cinnamon
- Raw honey

Directions:
1. Infuse each apple with raisins, spray cinnamon, sprinkle honey, get into air fryer and cook at 367°f for 17 minutes.
2. Allow to cool
3. Serve.

Nutrition:
Calories: 100, Protein: 0.55g, Fat: 0.33g, Carbs: 26.8g

239. Pumpkin Cookies

P Prep Time 25 m | P Cooking Time 15 m | 4 Servings

Ingredients
- 2 and ½ cups flour
- ½ tbsp. Baking soda
- 1 tbsp. Flax seed
- 3 tbsp. Water
- ½ cup pumpkin flesh
- ¼ cup honey
- 2 tbsp. Butter
- 1 tbsp. Vanilla extract
- ½ cup dark chocolate chips

Directions:
1. Mix flax seed with water in a bowl, turn and allow for a while.
2. Mix flour with baking soda and salt in another bowl.
3. Mix in honey with pumpkin puree, vanilla extract, flaxseed and butter in third bowl.
4. Blend flour with chocolate chips and honey mix and turn.
5. Measure 1 tablespoon of cookie dough on a lined baking sheet. Do same with remaining dough, get into air fryer and cook at 350° f for 15 minutes.
6. Allow to cool.
7. Serve.

Nutrition:
Calories: 72, Protein: 1.94g, Fat: 2.14g, Carbs: 11.36g

240. Figs And Coconut Butter Mix

P Prep Time 10 m | P Cooking Time 4 m | 3 Servings

Ingredient
- 2 tbsp. Coconut butter
- 12 figs
- ¼ cup sugar
- 1 cup almonds

Directions:
1. Melt butter in pan over medium heat.
2. Put figs, almonds and sugar. Toss, get into air fryer and cook at 300°f for 4 minutes.
3. Share into bowls then serve cold.

Nutrition:
Calories: 186, Protein: 1.27g, Fat: 8.19g, Carbs: 29.87g

241. Lemon Bars

P Prep Time 35 m | P Cooking Time 25 m | 6 Servings

Ingredients
- 4 eggs
- 2 ¼ cups flour
- Lemon juice
- 1 cup butter
- 2 cups sugar

Directions:
1 Mix ½ cup sugar with butter and 2 cups flour in a bowl, turn properly, push to the bottom of a pan, get into the fryer and cook at 350°f for 10 minutes.
2 Mix in remaining flour, with the remaining sugar, lemon juice and eggs, beat properly and sprinkle over crust.
3 Put in the fryer at 350°f for 15 minutes still, allow to cool, slice bars.
4 Serve.

Nutrition:
Calories: 660, Protein: 11.17g, Fat: 37.59g, Carbs: 70.28g

242. Orange Sponge Cake

P Prep Time 50 m | P Cooking Time 15 m | 6 Servings

Ingredients
- 9 oz sugar
- 9 oz self-rising flour
- 9 oz butter
- 3 eggs
- 1 tsp baking powder
- 1 tsp vanilla extract
- Zest of 1 orange

Frosting:
- 4 egg whites
- Juice of 1 orange
- 1 tsp orange food coloring
- Zest of 1 orange
- 7 oz superfine sugar

Directions
1 Preheat breville on bake function to 160 f and place all cake ingredients, in a bowl and beat with an electric mixer. Transfer half of the batter into a prepared cake pan; bake for 15 minutes. Repeat the process for the other half of the batter.
2 Meanwhile, prepare the frosting by beating all frosting ingredients together. Spread the frosting mixture on top of one cake. Top with the other cake.

Nutrition:
Calories: 828, Protein:11.46 g, Fat: 39.77g, Carbs: 107.89g

243. Cashew Bars

P Prep Time 25 m | P Cooking Time 15 m | 6 Servings

Ingredients
- 1/3 cup honey
- ¼ cup almond meal

- 1 tbsp. Almond butter
- 1 ½ cups cashews
- 4 dates
- ¾ cup coconut
- 1 tbsp. Chia seeds

Directions:

1 Mix honey with almond butter and almond meal in a bowl and turn properly.
2 Put coconut, dates, cashew and chia seeds and turn properly still.
3 Pour mix on a lined baking sheet and compress properly.
4 Get it in fryer and cook at 300° f for 15 minutes.
5 Allow to cool, slice into medium bars then serve.

Nutrition:

Calories: 483, Protein: 8.18g, Fat: 35.96g, Carbs: 39.44g

244. Fried Cream

P Prep Time 10-20 m | P Cooking Time 15-30 m | 8 Servings

Ingredients:

For the cream:

- 500 ml of whole milk
- 3 egg yolks
- 150 g of sugar
- 50 g flour
- 1 envelope Vanilla Sugar

Ingredients for the pie:

- 2 eggs
- Unlimited Breadcrumbs
- 1 tsp oil

Directions:

1 First prepare the custard; once cooked, pour the cream into a dish previously covered with a transparent film and level well. Let cool at room temperature for about 2 hours.
2 Grease the basket and distribute it all over.
3 When the cream is cold, place it on a cutting board and cut it into dice; Pass each piece of cream first in the breadcrumbs, covering the 4 sides well in the beaten egg and then in the pie.
4 Place each part inside the basket. Set the temperature to 1500C.
5 Cook for 10 to 12 minutes, turning the pieces after 6 to 8 minutes.
6 The doses of this cream are enough to make 2 or even 3 kitchens in a row.

Nutrition:

Calories 355, Fat 18.37g, Carbohydrates 44.94g, Sugars 30.36g, Protein 4.81g, Cholesterol 45mg

245. Apple, cream, and hazelnut crumble

P Prep Time 10-20 m | P Cooking Time 15-30 m | 6 Servings

Ingredients:

- 4 golden apples
- 100 ml of water
- 50g cane sugar
- 50g of sugar
- ½ tbsp cinnamon
- 200 ml of fresh cream

- Chopped hazelnuts to taste

Directions:

1 In a bowl, combine the peeled apples, cut into small cubes, cane sugar, sugar, and cinnamon.

2 Pour the apples inside the basket, add the water. Set the air fryer to 1800C and simmer for 15 minutes depending on the type of apple used and the size of the pieces.

3 At the end, divide the apples in the serving glasses, cover with previously whipped cream and sprinkle with chopped hazelnuts.

Nutrition:

Calories 828.8, Fat 44.8 g, Carbohydrate 120.6 g, Sugars54.2 g, Protein4.4 g , Cholesterol 29.5 mg

246. Fregolotta with hazelnuts

P Prep Time 10-20 m | P Cooking Time 15-30 m | 8 Servings

Ingredients:

- 200g of flour
- 150g of sugar
- 100 g melted butter
- 100g hazelnuts
- 1 egg
- ½ sachet of yeast

Directions:

1. Do not finely chop the hazelnuts. In a large bowl, pour all the ingredients (the butter once melted should be cooled before using), mix lightly, without the dough becoming too liquid.

2. Place parchment paper on the bottom of the basket and pour the mixture into it. Spread it evenly.

3. Set the air fryer to 1800C and simmer for 15 minutes and then turn the cake.

4. Cook for an additional 5 minutes.

5. Let cool and sprinkle the cake with icing sugar.

Nutrition:

Calories 465, Carbohydrates 37g, Fat 25g, Sugars 3g, Protein 20g, Cholesterol 0mg

247. Apple Treat With Raisins

P Prep Time 15 m | P Cooking Time 10 m | 4 Servings

Ingredients

- 2 apples, cored
- ½ oz almonds
- ¾ oz raisins
- 1 tbsp sugar

Directions

1. Preheat air fryer on bake function to 360 f and in a bowl, mix sugar, almonds, raisins. Blend the mixture using a hand mixer. Fill cored apples with the almond mixture. Place the prepared apples in your air fryer basket and cook for 10 minutes. Serve with powdered sugar.

Nutrition:

Calories: 188, Protein: 2.88g, Fat: 5.64g, Carbs: 35.63g

248. Almond Cookies With Dark Chocolate

P Prep Time 145 m | P Cooking Time 35 m | 4 Servings

Ingredients

- 1 egg whites

- ½ tsp almond extract
- ⅓ cups sugar
- ¼ tsp salt
- 1 tsp lemon juice
- 1 ½ tsp vanilla extract
- Melted dark chocolate to drizzle

Directions

2.   In a mixing bowl, add egg whites, salt, and lemon juice. Beat using an electric mixer until foamy. Slowly add the sugar and continue beating until completely combined; add the almond and vanilla extracts. Beat until stiff peaks form and glossy.

3.   Line a round baking sheet with parchment paper. Fill a piping bag with the meringue mixture and pipe as many mounds on the baking sheet as you can leaving 2-inch spaces between each mound.

4.   Place the baking sheet in the fryer basket and bake at 250 f for 5 minutes on bake function. Reduce the temperature to 220 f and bake for 15 more minutes. Then, reduce the temperature to 190 f and cook for 15 minutes. Remove the baking sheet and let the meringues cool for 2 hours. Drizzle with dark chocolate and serve.

Nutrition:

Calories: 170, Protein: 7.24g, Fat: 0.19g, Carbs: 34.06g

249. Air Fried Banana With Sesame Seeds

P Prep Time 15 m | P Cooking Time 8-10 m | 5 Servings

Ingredients

- ½ cups flour
- 2 bananas, sliced
- 1 tsp salt
- 1 tbsp sesame seeds
- 1 cup water
- 2 eggs, beaten
- 1 tsp baking powder
- ½ tbsp sugar

Directions

1.   Preheat air fryer on bake function to 340 f.

2.   In a bowl, mix salt, sesame seeds, flour, baking powder, eggs, sugar, and water. Coat sliced bananas with the flour mixture; place the prepared slices in the air fryer basket; cook for 8-10 minutes. Serve chilled.

Nutrition:

Calories: 327, Protein: 9.73g, Fat: 7.55g, Carbs: 57.33g

250. Vanilla Brownies With Chocolate Chips

P Prep Time 25 m | P Cooking Time 20 m | 2 Servings

Ingredients

- 1 whole egg, beaten
- ¼ cup chocolate chips
- 1 tbsp white sugar
- ⅓ cup flour
- 1 tbsp safflower oil
- 1 tsp vanilla

- ¼ cup cocoa powder

Directions

1. Preheat air fryer on bake function to 320 f and in a bowl, mix the beaten egg, sugar, oil, and vanilla. In another bowl, mix cocoa powder and flour. Add the flour mixture to the vanilla mixture and stir until fully incorporated. Pour the mixture into the baking pan and sprinkle chocolate chips on top. Cook for 20 minutes. Chill and cut into squares to serve.

Nutrition:

Calories: 321, Protein: 8.56g, Fat: 20.03g, Carbs: 30.78g

CPSIA information can be obtained
at www.ICGtesting.com
Printed in the USA
LVHW100733210221
679518LV00015B/879

9 781922 577436